Transparency

This book critiques the contemporary recourse to transparency in law and policy.

This is, ostensibly, the information age. At the heart of the societal shift toward digitalisation is the call for transparency and the liberalisation of information and data. Yet, with the recent rise of concerns such as 'fake news', post-truth and misinformation, where the policy responses to all these phenomena has been a petition for even greater transparency, it becomes imperative to critically reflect on what this dominant idea means, whom it serves, and what the effects are of its power. In response, this book provides the first sustained critique of the concept of transparency in law and policy. It offers a concise overview of transparency in law and policy around the world, and critiques how this concept works discursively to delimit other forms of governance, other ways of knowing and other realities. It draws on the work of Michel Foucault on discourse, archaeology and genealogy, together with later Foucaultian scholars, including Gayatri Chakravorty Spivak and Judith Butler, as a theoretical framework for challenging and thinking anew the history and understanding of what has become one of the most popular buzzwords of 21st century law and governance.

At the intersection of law and governance, this book will be of considerable interest to those working in these fields; but also to those engaged in other interdisciplinary areas, including society and technology, the digital humanities, technology laws and policy, global law and policy, as well as the surveillance society.

Rachel Adams is a Senior Research Specialist at the Human Sciences Research Council, South Africa, and a Post-Doctoral Researcher with the Information Law and Policy Centre, at the Institute of Advanced Legal Studies, University of London.

New Trajectories in Law

Series editors Adam Gearey, Birkbeck College, University of London
Colin Perrin, Commissioning Editor, Routledge

for information about the series and details of previous and forthcoming titles, see https://www.routledge.com/New-Trajectories-in-Law/book-series/NTL

Transparency
New Trajectories in Law

Rachel Adams

Routledge
Taylor & Francis Group

LONDON AND NEW YORK

First published 2020 by Routledge

2 Park Square, Milton Park, Abingdon, Oxon OX14 4RN

605 Third Avenue, New York, NY 10017

Routledge is an imprint of the Taylor & Francis Group, an informa business

First issued in paperback 2021

A glasshouse book

British Library Cataloguing-in-Publication Data
A catalogue record for this book is available from the British Library

Library of Congress Cataloging-in-Publication Data
Names: Adams, Rachel (Rachel Margaret) author.
Title: Transparency: new trajectories in law / Rachel Adams.
Description: Abingdon, Oxon; New York, NY: Routledge, 2020. |
Series: New trajectories in law | Based on author's thesis
(doctoral – University of Cape Town, Faculty of Law, 2017)
issued under title: The creation of 'a world after its own
image': a genealogy of transparency. |
Includes bibliographical references and index.
Identifiers: LCCN 2019057996 (print) | LCCN 2019057997 (ebook) |
ISBN 9780367346003 (hardback) | ISBN 9780429340819 (ebook)
Subjects: LCSH: Sociological jurisprudence. |
Disclosure of information. | Transparency in government. |
Human rights. | Technology and law.
Classification: LCC K370 .A33 2020 (print) |
LCC K370 (ebook) | DDC 340/.115–dc23
LC record available at https://lccn.loc.gov/2019057996
LC ebook record available at https://lccn.loc.gov/2019057997

ISBN: 978-0-367-34600-3 (hbk)
ISBN: 978-1-03-217553-9 (pbk)
DOI: 10.4324/9780429340819

Typeset in Times New Roman
by codeMantra

For my Grandmother, Janet Jackson

Contents

Acknowledgements

I am greatly indebted to a number of people whose support and guidance made this book possible. To my husband, Yazeed, for tirelessly engaging in conversations on the meanings of transparency and its place within our so-called information age, and my children – Iriyana, Ali and Iman – who generously shared their mother's attention with Michel Foucault and the many other giants whose shoulders I stood on to write this book.

I also wish to thank my mother for her unwavering love and for the many hours spent entertaining my young children so I could write; my parents-in-law and my father, who remains a constant source of inspiration and reassurance.

In addition, my gratitude extends to Fola Adeleke for introducing me to transparency and encouraging me to critique it, to Jaco Barnard-Naudé who supervised much of the research of this book during my doctoral studies at the University of Cape Town and to my colleagues Nora Ni Loideain, Temba Masilela and Stephen Rule for their sage advice and encouragement.

Some parts of this book have been previously published with *Critical Legal Thinking*, specifically:

R. Adams. 2017. Key Concept: Michel Foucault, Discourse. *Critical Legal Thinking.* Posted: 17th November 2017. Available from: http:// criticallegalthinking.com/2017/11/17/michel-foucault-discourse/. [Accessed 10 September 2019].

R. Adams. 2018. Did Baudrillard Foretell the Advent of Fake News? Critical Legal Thinking. Posted: 27th April 2018. Available from: http://criticallegalthinking.com/2018/04/27/did-baudrillard-foretell-the-advent-of-fake-news/. [Accessed 10 September 2019].

Kind permission has been granted for the re-use of these texts here.

Excerpt from *Unbelievable: Why we believe and why we don't*: © Graham Ward, 2014, I.B. Tauris. Used by permission of Bloomsbury Publishing Plc.

Excerpt from *Corporate Truth: The Limits to Transparency* by Adrian Henriques, 2007. Used by permission of Taylor and Francis.

Excerpt from *The Transparency of Evil*, by Jean Baudrillard, 2009. Used by permission of Verso Books.

Preface

My involvement with the idea of transparency began when I was working at the South African Human Rights Commission over 2012–2016. Within this context, transparency was presented as a human right embedded within the ambitious content of the right of access to information. It was considered to be a fundamental – if yet rather unrealised – ideal of the new democratic dispensation of South Africa. Broader literature on the subject echoed its value and necessity for a functioning democracy as well as for the ethical conduct of bodies, whether public or private. Indeed, "transparency" was being invoked across global society: from international human rights and good governance strategies, to anti-corruption efforts and investment. Global discourse had constructed transparency as a catch-all solution for a vast array of different undesirables within modern society. Yet, its construction as a human right and as an ethical principle meant that its socio-historical construction went by unnoticed: transparency was taken as a given.

From these emergent observations, I began to formulate the questions which would ultimately become the starting point for my PhD thesis and, ultimately, this book. Questions such as: how and why was the idea of transparency constructed? Who constructed it? What does its construction serve? And what are the perhaps unintended effects of this construction as it is put to work in different parts of the world today?

The work of Michel Foucault, and particularly that on discourse, stood out as a befitting framework for exploring these questions. Indeed, Foucault gave me a vocabulary with which to articulate my concerns about transparency; and his theories sparked new ways of thinking about and accounting for the global rise of the concept. I hope that in drawing from Foucault's oeuvre, I have not taken a positivist appropriation of his work, but have instead extended the scope of his focus onto an idea and discourse which I see as central to the global project of modernity.

The objective of this research, then, is not to weigh up the merits of transparency from a pseudo-objective position, as such a position is not possible; nor does it aim to dismiss the notion of transparency in its entirety or its usage within particular paradigms and industries of contemporary times. Indeed, I fully recognise that many transparency initiatives undertaken around the world have been done so in good faith, and not in an (conscious) effort to hegemonically dominate one world-view over another. And that efforts to create and enforce a standard of information transparency have generated many desirous effects and brought material benefit to many individuals and communities.

Rather, this book is concerned with bringing out the unconscious possibilities embedded within the discourse of transparency, deconstructing its claims and assumptions and problematising the making of transparency as a discourse of modernity. Indeed, its efforts are largely polemical: seeking to present the opposing side to the argument *for* transparency, which itself has been so well versed and appraised.

Introduction

The discourse of transparency

'Beginning with the things it produced'[1]

> What I would like to do [...] is to reveal a positive unconscious of
> knowledge: a level that eludes the consciousness of the scientist
> and yet is part of scientific discourse.
>
> (Foucault, 1989: xi)

In 2007, at the foot of the Athens Acropolis, a new building was
erected. Its geography positions the structure gazing up at the ancient
temples astride the top of the historic citadel, revering the wonders of
Greek antiquity. Within its construction, some of the most precious
and distinctive artefacts of ancient Greece are housed and put on dis-
play, including 50 metres of the Parthenon Frieze. Sheets of glass dominate the building's outward edifice, suggesting an invisible distinction
between the ancient and the modern. It has been named a 'temple to
transparency' (Gonchar, 2007).

The Acropolis Museum stands as a monumental symbol of the eminent value of transparency in modern Western society, where 'modernity' can be understood as naming the present teleological condition.
Note the preposition in the phrasing above: this is not a temple *of*
transparency, but a temple *to* transparency. Transparency is the object, the ultimate, the final referent. Transparency – far from being a
causative function that produces positive societal effects (as, we will
discuss, its narrative claims) – *is* the effect: it is itself the value to be
cherished and monumentalised.

The erection of the Acropolis Museum in the first decade of the new
millennium coincided with a global call for transparency. It was the
decade in which over 65 countries adopted access to information laws,
creating juridical precedents for transparency. It was the decade in
which the European Union adopted the two eminent transparency

directives to consolidate transparency within the Banking and Finance division of the European Commission. And it was the decade in which Barack Obama became the president of the United States on the strength of his promise for transparency.

Robert Schulzinger speaks of transparency as the 'buzz word' of the last decade (2011: 165). Aarti Gupta states that it is 'a key concept of our times' (2008: 1). While for Clare Birchall and Kristen Lord, we are living in an 'age of transparency' (2014: 78; 2006: 5). Indeed, transparency is a major feature of political campaigns across the world. It is lauded by big businesses as a corporate value of good governance. It is quoted as one of the key solutions to addressing opacity and discrimination within artificial intelligence (AI) systems. And with the establishment of multi-lateral government agencies designed to promote global transparency, such as the Open Government Partnership (OGP), the concept has gained unequalled, close to universal, status. That is, we simply accept transparency as something good, something ethical in itself that will, in turn, bring about societal benefits, such as accountability, civic participation and even a rebalancing of power/knowledge asymmetries.

In all, transparency is now an institutionalised and dominant value of modern society. While it denotes the disclosure of information, particularly by a powerful group or institution, it more widely suggests a way of behaving such that one's actions and decisions are open to inspection by others. Through the generalised rise of transparency as a value of modern society, it has become, I will argue here, what Garcia-Jerez would describe as 'naturalised discourse', that is, discourse that is 'commonsensical even though it has actually been framed by the values and beliefs of a given social group' (2016: 1). That transparency can be understood as a discourse – following both Garcia-Jerez and, more closely, Michel Foucault (1970, 1971, 1972, 1989) – is one of the central tenets of this book and will be explored in detail over the following chapters.

Yet, transparency – central to the call for openness and the greater liberalisation of information in all areas of social and political life today – seems to be on the brink of undoing itself. As efforts to increase transparency by promulgating the production, disclosure and dissemination of information of all kinds through every conceivable channel meet with digitalisation – in the form of social media and internet and data technologies – what has arisen are two key informational crises. The first relates to the rise of issues such as post-truth, the attention economy, 'fake news' and deep fakes, which all expose the fallacy of transparency's underlying assumption that information disclosed would be true. The second concerns privacy. With the rapid advancement of data-based technologies and algorithmic processing, data – and particularly personal data – has become a key currency of what Shoshana Zuboff has named the age of surveillance capitalism. These technologies rely on the real-time appropriation of massive amounts of data in order to generate and maintain the accuracy of its analytics and decision-making, whether for financial forecasting, intelligence gathering or online advertising and product placement. Data is gathered through an increasing range of connected devices in spaces both public – such as CCTV cameras, or contactless payment systems – and private, including social media accounts, driverless cars or AI-driven home assistants. Within these contexts, the disclosure of personal information is fuelled through increasingly opaque disciplinary technologies, including click-wrap privacy agreements and, more generally, through a dominant world view which encourages individual transparency under the rubric of social sharing.

Yet, just when it seems that the call for transparency has perhaps gone too far, when instead of open and accountable institutions we face the loss of privacy and the generation of information we can no longer decipher as true or not, calls for transparency again reverberates in the policy responses to these very informational crises its discourse arguably helped produce. In the face of steep privacy concerns and the spread of misinformation through digital technologies, the response is simply that we need more and better transparency. In this book, I explore this conundrum as – what I call – the post-transparent. In this post-transparency, the notion of transparency no longer refers to its supposed original purpose and objective of making institutions visible in order to make them accountable. Instead, transparency functions as a form of power, at the level of citizens and individual subjectivity, to mete out unwanted behaviour, producing a homogeneity whose behaviour and even affectations can be anticipated, controlled and capitalised, all under the rubric of a transparent society whose intentions and actions are – on account of its supposed transparency – legible to all.

The discourse of transparency

As Frederick Schauer aptly puts it, 'transparency, it appears these days, is everywhere; or at least *talk* of it is everywhere' (my emphasis, 2011: 1340). It is indeed striking that the idea of transparency has been so readily adopted within such varied contexts, and by such diverse actors. Claims to transparency now proliferate in countless forms and circumstances, including tax transparency, corporate transparency as a feature of good governance, transparency in political campaigns, transparency in Parliament, open budgets and fiscal transparency, open data, world aid transparency, transparency in company ownership, disclosure of interest transparency, algorithmic transparency and publish what you pay campaigns – to name just a few. Institutions promoting transparency – which range from the Bretton Woods institutions to local governments, and from corporations to international non-government organisations (INGOs) – all perpetuate the rhetorical power of transparency through the incessant reaffirmation of its claims, objectives and central 'truths'. Claims such as: "transparency promotes accountability"; "transparency promotes democracy"; "transparency allows us to participate in decision-making"; "transparency allows us to see and understand the forces of power that act upon us"; "transparency gives us the truth"; "a transparent institution is trustworthy"; "transparency is a universal value"; "transparency is about inclusivity"; "to be transparent is morally right" and "those that are transparent have nothing to hide".

Through these claims, transparency is able to continually reiterate and re-perform its symbolic terms. Foucault would describe these re-iterations of the value and meaning of transparency as 'commentaries' (1972: 221). Commentaries, he notes, circulate within the paradigm of the discourse, repeatedly enunciating its own internal meaning with the effect of spreading the discursive force of its claims, and forever extending the parameters of its discursive control. Through mediated processes of dissemination, discourse in general, and the transparency discourse in particular, indeed seems to spread, as an intricate part of globalisation, like an ever–expanding web all over the planet. It is these commentaries which together form the discursive archive of my analysis here, and whose rise and claims I seek to problematise.

Thus, this short book is about transparency, and specifically, how transparency is spoken about and its effects. I analyse the global rise and dominance of transparency, particularly as it features in law and policy, where its status is inherently legitimated by the formal structures in which it lies. I seek to critique transparency as a dominant discourse, analysing the assumptions upon which it rests and the claims that it makes. I explore the perhaps unintended power-effects of the discourse of transparency and look to reveal the hidden realities existent within and resultant from it. Within this context, following Foucault, I take 'discourse' to refer to a way of organising knowledge and producing meaning that structures the constitution of social relations through the collective understanding of the discursive logic and the acceptance of the discourse as social fact. At its most basic, I read Foucault's work on discourse as a technique of problematisation. Thus, by problematising the statements and claims of the transparency discourse, the supposedly natural and fixed meanings of this concept can be opened up, and the effects of power that this discourse produces can be explored.

In identifying these statements and claims, I aim to account for how transparency was 'put into discourse',[2] and analyse the ways in which it gains its discursive power. I argue that modern transparency is constituted as a social fact and ethical value, and that through its truth statements it both creates and reproduces its power, working to shape the social and global reality in which it exists. To this end, the transparency discourse legitimises regimes of power and subjectivities which claim to be transparent, and in doing so, delimits and excludes other forms of governance, ways of knowing and ways of being that do not have a claim to transparency or do not follow transparency's prescriptions, particularly as they may appear in the Global South. Yet, as transparency marks out its subjects from the darkness, it not only excludes them from its discourse – for as Foucault reminds us 'none shall enter the order of discourse [...] if he is not, from the outset, qualified to do so' (1981: 62) – but also *contains* them within its homogenising gaze. This gaze seeks first to create the illusion of a simplified, accessible and legible world, and second, to normalise the information economy where those places and people at the forefront of the production and collection of information can thrive, and where others have transparency or disclosure forced upon them such that the status quo can continue uninterrupted.

Transparency in scholarship

Despite its dominance as a doctrinal value of the information age, 'transparency' as a concept has received little critical attention, remaining vague and broadly undefined. One of the most commonly invoked narratives is that transparency concerns the disclosure of information by a particular entity with the view to increasing the visibility and accountability of this entity to a broader spectrum of persons or institutions. Some of the key scholars in the field have endeavoured to articulate a more precise definition of this concept, with Lord, for example, writing that 'transparency is a condition in which information about the priorities, intentions, capabilities, and behaviour of powerful organizations is widely available to the global public' (2006: 5).

The leading thinking on transparency is that it engenders an array of societal benefits, including the enhancement of democracy and accountability, as noted above. Yet, much of the literature on transparency both implicitly and explicitly works to promote the concept, by simply listing its numerous organisational and societal benefits, without scepticism. Quoted benefits – besides promoting democracy and accountability – is that transparency enhances trust in organisations through improving organisational legitimacy; increasing profits or performance – including, by strengthening investor relations; advancing decision-making, organisational culture and good governance through information disclosure and decreasing opportunities for corruption. More recently, the discourse on trust has been appropriated to information technology and data systems, and much fervour has gone into efforts to increase public trust in such technologies, particularly in response to concerns around privacy and data protection. Transparency remains a central policy feature for attaining trust in technology and the powers that use it. In general, however, the value and meaning of transparency is taken as a given.

Somewhat more critically, Cary Coglianese warns that with regard to government transparency, there can be 'too much of a good thing' (2009: 520). Coglianese's assumption is that government transparency is undoubtedly beneficial, yet points out that it should not be applied without discretion which, he notes, would inevitably risk public disappointment and cynicism if transparency was not able to achieve what it claimed to. Together with the work of transparency scholars such as Slaughter and Hale, and Meijer and Lord, this corpus of scholarship broadly considers transparency's over-ambitious nature, yet leaves the concept itself largely unexplored.

For Mark Fenster, there is an inherent tension between what transparency seeks to achieve, and how the concept has been constructed within law, and particularly access to information laws (2017). Fenster, too, hints that part of transparency's power has been achieved through the way it is socially imagined – what I speak of here as the way it is spoken about. He writes that 'transparency's symbolic pull, its ability to grab the public's imagination with the image of Ali Baba's treasure trove of secrets, leads us to fetishize means without fully considering the ends they are intended to reach and without attempting to grapple with the question of why these means always prove unsatisfactory' (2017: 9). It is precisely the tension between what transparency – and Fenster's focus here is specifically on government transparency – claims it will achieve, and what its impact on democratic governance and visible accountability has actually been, that Fenster seeks to explore.

Indeed, transparency scholars have been quick to note that a high degree of nebulousness surrounds transparency. Hood and Heald's assertion in 2006 that 'transparency is more often preached than practised, more often referred to than defined, and more often advocated than critically analysed' (2006: 3) remains markedly true, with Robert G Vaughn and Padideh Ala'i noting in 2014 that 'in the last two decades, transparency has become a ubiquitous, but stubbornly ambiguous, term' (2014:1). More recently, Emmanuel Alloa and Dieter Thomä have polemically stated that 'nothing is less clear than what exactly is meant when the word "transparency" is used' (2018: 2).

While transparency's meaning today remains somewhat obscure, historical critiques of the concept reveal that in other times and places, the ideas was treated with suspicion. In a comprehensive treatise on the subject in post-war France, Stefanos Geroulanos investigates the mistrust of transparency by leading thinkers, from Jean-Paul Satre to Calude Leford. Geroulanos describes this suspicion of transparency as follows:

> It held up a false mirror to the self, to society, to knowledge, proffering a misguided belief in the purity of the self. The world was not transparency, because it was complex, layered, structured, filled with heterogeneity. To appeal to transparency and related ideas was to pretend that this complexity did not exist'.
>
> (2017: 10)

Geroulanos' work provides a critical touchstone for revisiting critical perspectives on transparency and for thinking through what the effects of the idealisation of this notion in society today may be. For, as Laurence Lessig has so keenly articulated, within today's society, to critique transparency has become implicitly considered wrongful and inapropos: 'who can be against transparency?' he asks, 'its virtues are so crushingly obvious' (2009: 1). It is precisely against this dogmatism in which the idea of transparency sits, that this book seeks to make its contribution, and explore the iniquities it perhaps unwittingly produces.

Book outline

This book is structured in three parts over six main chapters. Part I examines the history and discursive rise of transparency, from the designs of the Palace of the League of Nations in the 1920s (Chapter 1), through to the proliferation of access to information laws in the early

2000s (Chapter 2) and the corresponding emphasis on transparency at an international level (Chapter 3). I argue that the discursive power of transparency rests on its historical association to the Enlightenment; its claims to inclusivity, neutrality, universality and trust and jurisprudentially, its affiliation with notions of human rights. These claims work to legitimise the idea of transparency itself, and those places, institutions and individuals which assert its value. But, as the discourse legitimises those with a claim to transparency, it also excludes and renders illegitimate those who do not make a similar claim, including, as I examine here, other forms of governance that are not necessarily 'transparent'. I refer to this as the 'epistemic violence' of transparency, as derived from Gayatri Chakravorty Spivak's seminal essay, 'Can the Subaltern Speak?' (Chapters 2 and 3). This book therefore explores how the discourse of transparency, which sets the concept up as a universal and inclusive ethical value, works to delimit other realities, for example – other kinds of knowledge and information that do not conform to the strictures of 'records' set out in access to information laws (Chapters 2 and 3). Together, the delimitations set out by the discourse of transparency stigmatise that which is hidden, unseen or secret, with significant implications for subjectivity and, as is more typically discussed, privacy.

Accordingly, Part II explores and critiques the two identified informational crises, noted above, that have arisen in the wake of the call for ever more transparency, openness and information production and disclosure: surveillance and the loss of privacy, on the one hand, and fake news, on the other hand. Thus, Chapter 5 engages with the notions of fake news, deep fakes and the attention economy, and the policy responses of the European Union, in particular, which call for further transparency as a key measure for addressing such concerns. I consider the foreboding critique of Jean Baudrillard on the hyper-information society, and how digitalisation has sent the transparency project haywire.

Chapter 6 turns to explore how the discourse of transparency has become ingrained on the bodies of those asked, demanded or implicitly coerced into self-disclose. From describing the normalising effects of surveillance, the chapter moves on to develop a critique of the self-disclosure hailed through a number of legislative regimes, including whistleblowing laws, legislation to ban the veil and surveillance laws, engaging with Foucault's ideas around the internalisation of discourse.

Part III, and the last chapter of this book, looks at how the discourse of transparency has, and can be, resisted. I engage in a sustained analysis of Foucault's notion of resistance as a counter to the disciplinary technologies of power and its effects on the subject, noting that this aspect of his theory remained somewhat under-examined. In exploring how the discourse of transparency has been resisted, I examine – among others issues – the right to be forgotten, provided for under the European Union General Data Protection Regulation (GDPR, 2016), as well as some of Clare Birchall's work on secrecy and opacity.

Approach: the order of discourse

This book draws on Foucaultian thought as a 'method' for examining the construct of transparency, and its power-effects. I use the term 'method' cautiously, aware of Foucault's apprehension of unified theories which discount the discontinuities and differences which he so pointedly seeks to make manifest. Nonetheless, this book engages with a broad selection of Foucault's work, including the lecture series at the College de France in the late 1970s–1980s that have been published posthumously. More specifically, the key Foucaultian concept which I engage with here is that of discourse, a central element of his oeuvre. Foucault appropriated the term to denote a historically contingent social system that produces knowledge and meaning, such that they constitute what he calls 'practices that systematically form the objects of which they speak' (1972: 49). Discourse is, thus, a way of organising knowledge that structures the constitution of social (and progressively global) relations through the collective understanding of the discursive logic and the acceptance of the discourse as social fact, as described above.

Discourses are produced by effects of power within a social order, and this power prescribes particular rules and categories which define the criteria for legitimating knowledge and truth within the discursive order: in short, what can and cannot be said according to the terms of the discourse. For transparency, this might be that "transparency promotes accountability" can be said, but "transparency is evil" cannot.[3] These rules and categories are considered *a priori*; that is, coming before the discourse. It is in this way that discourse masks its own construction and capacity to produce knowledge and meaning. It is also in this way that discourse claims an irrefutable a–historicity.

Through the reiteration of the symbolic terms of discourse as it is spoken in society, the meanings of ideas and notions that are part of that discourse become fixed. As this takes place, other meanings and interpretations become disqualified – immediately forbidden from entering discourse. Foucault speaks of this discursive process as reducing the contingencies (the other meanings) of text, in order to eliminate the differences which could challenge or destabilise the meaning and power of the discourse:

> In every society the production of discourse is at once controlled, selected, organised and redistributed by a certain number of procedures whose role is to ward off its powers and dangers, to gain mastery over its chance events, to evade its ponderous, formidable materiality.
>
> (1970: 53)

It is through this reiterative process that a discourse normalises and homogenises. By fixing the meaning of text, and by pre-determining the categories of reason by which statements are accepted as knowledge, a discourse creates an epistemic reality and becomes a technique of control and discipline. That which does not conform to the enunciated truth of discourse is rendered deviant, that is, outside of discourse, and outside of society, sociality or the 'sociable'. With effect, Foucault demonstrated these discursive practices of exclusion in the categories of reason and madness in his first major work, *Madness and Civilisation*.

However, it is in one of his last published works – *The Will to Knowledge: History of Sexuality Volume I* – that we find a compelling description of the function of discourse analysis as a technique of critique and problematisation. With respect to the discourse of sexuality, Foucault asks what the effects of power are of what has been said under this discourse and remarks that the task at hand is

> to account for the fact that it is spoken about, to discover who does the speaking, the positions and viewpoints from which they speak, the institutions which prompt people to speak about it and which store and distribute the things that are said.
>
> (1998: 11)

Ultimately, Foucault seeks to understand how sex was 'put into discourse' (1998: 11). What Foucault sets out here is the task of discourse analysis. It must 'account for the fact that [the discourse in question] is spoken about' and analyse the effects of power that are produced by what is said. Moreover, discourse analysis must seek to unfix and destabilise the accepted meanings of the discourse, and to reveal the ways in which dominant discourses exclude, marginalise and oppress realities that constitute, at least, equally valid claims to the question of how power could and should be exercised.

In addition to discourse, this book also adapts aspects of Foucault's ideas on genealogy and archaeology, which constitute historical analytics, that is, tools for conducting alternative histories of an idea or concept. Foucault's work on genealogy – which became dominant after 1970 – arose as a revised historic-analytic to 'archaeology', a concept which largely defined his oeuvre up until this point. Similar, yet markedly distinct, both concepts emanate out of what Jeffrey Nealon articulates as 'Foucault's repeated emphasis on material conditions of emergence rather than philosophical conditions of possibility' (1996: 430). Indeed, Foucault emphasises his rejection of historical practices which seek affirmations of transcendental truth and subjectivity in both *Archaeology of Knowledge* (in which Foucault sets out the archaeological method) and his essay of 1971 'Nietzsche, Genealogy, History' (where Foucault most clearly articulates his concept of genealogy). Thus, Foucault – in keeping with his reading of Nietzsche – refutes the 'search for 'origins'': a historical method which seeks to preserve the 'telos of mankind' (1972: 13) and reveal 'the image of a primordial truth fully adequate to its nature' (1971: 78). Indeed, it is this insistence of a single unified truth which is so problematic for, as Rudi Visker explains, 'the search for an origin – even for one that is irretrievably lost – simultaneously meant the promise of its return' (1995: 30). In the hope for the return of the 'truth', other truths and other possibilities are denied: this 'truth' becomes delimiting. And in the insistence of the transcendence of 'truth', its construction is concealed. Within the archaeological 'method', the construction of truth takes place through discourse; within the genealogical, Foucault observes the construction of truth in the forces of power – the struggles and antagonisms – at play in particular historical events, in moments of discontinuity and transformation.

While I draw on the archaeological method as an analytical tool in the earlier chapters of this book (particularly Chapters 2, 3 and 4), the broader aim of this book is more closely genealogical. Indeed, I seek not only to examine the construction of the transparency discourse, but also how this construction is put to work as a régime of truth, claiming universality and inclusivity, among others, as well as how it functions in the production of subjectivity. In an interview, Foucault states that,

> I take care not to dictate how things should be. I try instead to pose problems, to make them active, to display them in such a complexity that they can silence the prophets and lawgivers, all those who speak for others or to others.

(2000: 288)

It is as such that I wish to critique transparency.

Summary

In short, this book seeks to interrupt the ostensible unity of the discourse of transparency as it appears around the world, and thus to demonstrate its historical contingency, showing that the idea is not an inevitable reality and can be, and has been, resisted. In doing so, I aim to deepen and make more complex the contemporary meaning of transparency by bringing about scepticism and allowing the concept to find fuller expression. Overall, this book aims to reveal what Foucault would call the 'positive unconscious' of transparency (1989: xi), that is, *that which lies beneath* the popular discourse of transparency: the structures of power, systems of exclusion, foreclosure of other possibilities and constructions of subjectivity that are inherent in the making and remaking of transparency as a discursive fact.

Notes

1 Phrase is taken from Foucault (1971: 93), where he speaks of Platonic modalities of history, stating that: '[t]his historical trait should not be founded on a philosophy of history, but dismantled, beginning with the things it produced'.
2 Phrase taken from Foucault (1988: 11): '[w]hat is at issue, briefly, is the over-all 'discursive fact', the way in which sex is 'put into discourse''.
3 I use this phrase in reference to a polemical and radical treatise on transparency written by Jean Baudrillard (1993) entitled *The Transparency of Evil: Essays on Extreme Phenomena*.

Further reading

Alloa, E., & Thoma, D. (eds). 2018. *Transparency, Society and Subjectivity: Critical Perspectives*. Basingstoke: Palgrave.
Baudrillard, J. 1993. *The Transparency of Evil: Essays on Extreme Phenomena*. Trans. J. Benedict. London: Verso.
Birchall, C. 2014. Radical Transparency? *Cultural Studies – Critical Methodologies* 14(1): 77–88.
Birchall, C. 2018. *Shareveillance: The Dangers of Openly Sharing and Covertly Collecting Data*. Minnesota: University of Minnesota Press.
Coglianese, C. 2009. The Transparent President? The Obama Administration and Open Government. *Governance* 22: 529–544.
Fenster, M. 2017. *The Transparency Fix: Secrets, Leaks and Uncontrollable Government Information*. Stanford, CA: Stanford University Press.
Foucault, M. 1970. The Order of Discourse. In R. Young. (ed). *Untying the Text: A Post-Structuralist Reader*. London: Routledge: pp. 48–78.

Foucault, M. 1971. Nietzsche, Genealogy, History. In P. Rabinow (ed). *The Foucault Reader*. New York: Pantheon Books, pp. 76–100.

Foucault, M. 1972. *Archaeology of Knowledge and the Discourse on Language*. Trans. A. M. Sheridan Smith. New York: Pantheon Books.

Foucault, M. 1989. *The Order of Things*. London: Routledge.

Foucault, M. 1998. *The Will to Knowledge: The History of Sexuality Volume 1*. Trans. R. Hurley. New York: Pantheon Books.

Foucault, M. 2000. An Interview with Michel Foucault. In M. Foucault (ed). *Power: Essential Works of Foucault 1954–1984 Volume 3*. Trans. R. Hurley & Others. New York: The New Press, pp. 239–297.

Garcia-Jerez, M. E. 2016. Naturalized Discourse in Arguments: A Textual Approach to the Study of Social Representations. *International Journal of Humanities, Arts and Social Sciences* 1(2): 1–9.

Garsten, C. & de Montoya, M. L. (eds). 2008. *Transparency in a New Global Order: Unveiling Organizational Visions*. Chelterham: Edward Elgar Publishing.

Geroulanos, S. 2017. *Transparency in Postwar France: A Critical History of the Present*. Stanford, CA: Stanford University Press.

Gonchar, J. 2007. A Temple to Transparency Rises in Athens. 19 June 2007. Architectural Record. Available from: http://archrecord.construction.com/tech/techFeatures/0706feature-1.asp. [5 August 2019].

Gupta, A. 2008. Transparency Under Scrutiny: Information Disclosure in Global Environmental Governance. *Global Environmental Politics* 8(2): 1–7.

Hale, T. N., & Slaughter, A. 2006. Transparency: Possibilities and Limitations. *The Fletcher Forum of World Affairs* 30(1): 153–164.

Han, B. 2012. *The Transparency Society*. Trans. E. Butler. Stanford, CA: Stanford University Press.

Hood, C., & Heald, D. (eds). 2006. *Transparency: The Key to Better Governance?* Oxford: Oxford University Press.

Lessig, L. 2009. Against Transparency. *The New Republic* 1.

Lord, K. 2006. *The Perils and Promise of Global Transparency: Why the Information Revolution May Not Lead to Security, Democracy, or Peace*. New York: State University of New York Press.

Nealon, J. T. 1996. Between Emergence and Possibility: Foucault, Derrida, and Judith Butler on Performative Identity. *Philosophy Today* 40(30): 430–439.

Pasquale, F. 2015. *The Blackbox Society: The Secret Algorithms that Control Money and Information*. Cambridge, MA: Harvard University Press.

Regulation (European Union). 2016. 2016/679 of the European Parliament and of the Council of 27 April 2016 on the Protection of Natural Persons with Regard to the Processing of Personal Data and on the Free Movement of Such Data, and Repealing Directive 95/46/EC [2016] OJ L119/1 (GDPR).

Roberts, A. 2006. *Blacked Out: Government Secrecy in the Information Age*. Cambridge: Cambridge University Press.

Schauer, F. 2011. Transparency in Three Dimensions. *University of Illinois Law Review* 4: 1339–1358.

Schulzinger, R. D. 2011. Presidential Address: Transparency, Secrecy and Citizenship. *Diplomatic History* 25: 165–178.

Vaugn, R. G., & Ala'i, P. (eds). *Research Handbook on Transparency*. Cheltenham: Edward Elgar Publishing.

Visker, R. 1995. Michel Foucault: Genealogy as Critique. Trans. C. Turner. Cambridge: Cambridge University Press.

Zuboff, S. 2018. *The Age of Surveillance Capitalism: The Fight for a Human Future at the New Frontier of Power*. London: Profile Books.

Part I

The discourse of transparency

1 A brief history of transparency's entry into discourse

Introduction

The word "transparency" first emerged in the 18th Century in relation to print and photography. It denoted the medium through which light refraction could take place in the production of an image. Those who spoke of it would have been small in number, engaged in what would then have been a highly technical endeavour. Today, transparency has become popularised and entrenched in modern discourse, spoken in almost every corner of the world, and in a broad range of settings. How did it get here? How did the idea of "transparency" come to represent an institutional value and a public good to trump all others? And how and why was the meaning of transparency displaced from its literal application as a see-through medium to a metaphor for political openness?

This chapter addresses these questions by tracing the evolution and diachronic rise of the concept of transparency, from the camera lens and the use of transparency in the designs for the Palace of the League of Nations, through to its association with human rights. This history is continued in Chapters 2 and 3 which examine in further detail the more recent formulations of transparency in terms of access to information laws (Chapter 2) and open government (Chapter 3). In doing so, I draw on the critical analytics developed by Foucault as tools for which to conduct alternative histories of an idea, which I set out in the first section below. I critique here the given history of the concept as an Enlightenment value, evident in scholarship on the history of transparency as well as implicitly embedded in the philosophical assumptions that underlie it. Yet, transparency's alignment to notions of freedom and rights has allowed the concept to become naturalised, that is, accepted as fact; it is part of the way things are, and therefore unquestionable. Recall Laurence Lessig's rhetorical question: 'who can be against transparency?' (2009: 1).

Moreover, transparency's suggestion of being a neutral and universal idea is embedded within its present-day metaphorical construction. Having traced its history, this chapter turns to engage with the problematics of its metaphorical use today. I explore how, as a metaphor, the claims made by the transparency narrative are fundamentally rhetorical, bearing significance and meaning only within the logic of its own discourse, although with profoundly material effects. Moreover, through its metaphorical construction, transparency makes a critical claim to truth and to not altering the information it discloses. I explore how these claims work to heighten the position of transparency as a neutral value.

Archaeology

Foucault's concept of archaeology, set out in detail in one of his earlier books *Archaeology of Knowledge*, can be understood as an analytical tool for uncovering alternative, interrupted, histories of systems of thought and knowledge – or, more generally, ideas (1972). The archaeological "method" suggests an unstructuring of accepted knowledge and the categories in which to describe its historical experience. *Archaeology of Knowledge* was not Foucault's most well-received work, criticised for establishing in structural and positivist terms an approach which sought to vehemently reject such things. Nevertheless, the book dedicates significant space to questioning the propositions of traditional history, incessantly discarding the teleological efforts of traditional historians and rejecting historical narratives which seek to create linear continuities between past and present. Foucault critiques the search for affirmations of transcendental human consciousness (also spoken of as *"urdoxa"*), echoing a critique put forward by Friedrich Nietzsche on self-comforting narratives, that is, the idea that we create narratives about the world to reinforce our central place and purpose within it – an idea that becomes important for thinking about the strategic value of the discourse of transparency.

Instead, Foucault (like Georges Canguilhem and Gaston Bachelard before him) calls for the displacement of the subject as the object of history, proffering archaeology as an alternative mode of history that holds discourse (rather than man) as its object of study. Foucault substantiates his framework by defining and discussing a series of interrelated concepts that constitute the archaeological method of discursive investigation, including 'commentary' (as noted in the Introduction to this book), 'statements' – defined, in its simplest form, as a singular unit of discourse, such as "transparency leads to accountability", and the 'archive', that constitutes the historical collective of statements and commentaries within a discourse and which becomes the focus of critique for the archaeologist. Thus, the archaeological method constitutes the uncovering of historical statements and an analysis of the rules and systems of thought which govern their coming into discourse, set alongside a critique of its given history. This "method" informs the approach to the analysis of the history of transparency set out below.

Transparency, the enlightenment and human rights

The given history of transparency – as set out by transparency scholars such as Meijer (2013) and Björkstrand and Mustonen (2006) – is that the concept arose from the Enlightenment ideals of the 18th century, and the way of ordering knowledge – what Foucault would call the episteme (a term he used to describe the structure of knowledge within a given historical period (1989)) – it ushered in. Stefanos Geroulanos, in his history of the concept of transparency in French thought, notes that Jean-Jacques Rousseau, one of the foremost thinkers of the Enlightenment, notably promoted what Geroulanos calls 'the modern idealization of transparency' (2017: 8) through his moralised commitment to the concept. But, in addition, one of the most significant consequences of the Enlightenment was the establishment of human rights as an ideal of human society.

In short, the Enlightenment can be understood as the Western period of discovery of pre-formed transcendental truths – *a priori* knowledge – which improved the life of humankind as a species-Being, occurring during the 18th Century in Western Europe. The Enlightenment rested upon the Kantian assertion that there existed regulative and pre-formed transcendental human ideas, revealed through the appropriation of reason, and providing the conditions for the possibility of all human knowledge, morality and freedom. More broadly, the Enlightenment is considered to have prompted our contemporary teleological modernity, and as noted above, notions of human rights and civil liberties. The first human rights declaration – Declaration of the Rights of Man and of the Citizen – arose in France in 1789 following the French Revolution. This formative human rights agreement incorporated two key provisions which related to ideas around transparency. These included the first human rights provision for a right to freedom of expression which stated that 'the free communication of ideas and opinions is one of the most precious of the rights of man' (Article 11), as well as Article 15 which read that 'every community has a right to demand of all its agents an account of their conduct'.

The right to freedom of expression, and the corollary responsibility upon the press, as the fourth estate, to realise this right, forms a central part of the given history of the concept of transparency as denoting the right of access to information (see also Fenster, 2017). Article 11 of the Declaration of the Rights of Man and of the Citizen developed into Article 19 of first the Universal Declaration of Human Rights (UDHR) in 1948 and then Article 19 of the International Covenant on Civil and Political Rights in 1966. However, it was not until 2006 that the right of access to information was expressly recognised until international human rights law as distinct right, derived from the right to freedom of expression in the Inter-American Court of Human Rights judgement in the matter of *Reyes v Chile*. Despite this, the idea of freedom of information had received broad attention far earlier as a principle for healthy international relations. Following World War II, foreign state transparency was promoted for the benefit of global media reporting in an effort to ensure that the tragedies of the War could not happen again. In 1946 the United Nations held an International Conference on Freedom of Information, at which the establishment of a Convention on Freedom of Information was discussed. In the preamble to the UN General Assembly Resolution calling for the conference, the importance and meaning of freedom of information as a human right was laid out:

> Freedom of information is a fundamental human right and is the touchstone of all the freedoms to which the United Nations is consecrated;
> Freedom of information implies the right to gather, transmit and publish news anywhere and everywhere without letters. As such it is an essential factor in any serious effort to promote the peace and progress of the world;
> Freedom of information requires as an indispensable element the willingness and capacity to employ its privileges without abuse. It requires as a basic discipline the moral obligation to seek the facts without prejudice and to spread knowledge without malicious intent;
> Understanding and co-operation among nations are impossible without an alert and sound world opinion which, in turn, is wholly dependent upon freedom of information.

(1947)

Embedded within this text, which notably came before the establishment of the UDHR, are some of the early normative assumptions and hopes for what transparency – at that point freedom of information – would engender. In particular, it was conceived of as a 'fundamental human rights' and, more so, as the touchstones of all the other freedoms and rights the UN at that point sought to enshrine. Moreover, freedom of information was decreed to be a 'moral obligation' upon which peace between nations is 'wholly dependent', suggesting that transparency was a central part of the new world order that international human rights – as a universal and moral legal code – sought to bring about. These are significant and far-reaching claims, and arguably the beginning of what was to become an evangelical campaign for transparency that characterised much of the 20th and early 21st centuries, as described by Mark Fenster (2017).

But, like the freedom-seeking narratives of the Enlightenment, human rights claim a particular inclusivity, universalism and morality that transcend both law and politics. Together with other related Enlightenment truths and values, human rights were considered *a priori*, universal, moral values: applicable to all humankind, everywhere. As will be discussed over the course of the next three chapter, in its alignment to human rights and Enlightenment values, transparency discursively sets itself outside of history, refusing to be assigned to any particular author or ideology, and in doing so, masking its political rationalities. Moreover, transparency's claim to originate from the Enlightenment legitimises its modern construction, supporting its status as an indisputable public good and, in the words of Ann Florini, a 'moral imperative' (1999: 2).

The given history of transparency as arising from the Enlightenment is taken as unproblematic, presenting the concept as naturalised: part of the ways things are and should be. Foucault cautions us against ideas and values that have become too dominant, that are unquestioned and accepted within the social fabric as convention. For these values conceal their political construction and normalise society, excluding and delimiting other realities.

Indeed, uncritically aligning transparency to the Enlightenment fails to take into account one of the key problematics of this historical moment, that the Enlightenment was a distinctly Western historical moment. Not only did it centre in the West, but it was premised upon, and proceeded to consolidate and strengthen, a Western epistemology largely based on the immediacy between seeing and knowing. Transparency arises directly from this epistemology, for the etymological roots of the word 'transparency' can be traced to the Latin 'trāns' – through or beyond, and 'pāreō' – to appear, with transparency therefore denoting *to appear through*, or *to make visible*. Indeed, the early IMF Working Group on Transparency defined transparency as a mechanism for making institutions 'accessible, visible and understandable' (1998). And indeed, today, transparency falls within a broader semantic field of visibility and light, which includes: 'sunlight', 'sunshine laws', 'oversight', 'observation', 'surveillance' and 'the invisible hand' (see here Florini, 1999). Yet this Enlightenment borne epistemology works to foreclose other epistemological realities, and particularly, fostered a distrust of those ideas and values antithetical to its own, including notions of darkness and secrecy. The place of transparency within this epistemological framework, where material visibility and objectivity are the key determinants of rationality, knowledge and truth, will be explored below.

Designing transparency

As noted in the beginning of this chapter, the word "transparency" first referred to the lens of a camera, denoting a physical property in the creation of an image. Jonathon Crary identifies the cameras as a paradigmatic technology, ushering in a new and dominant criterion for the acceptance of a proposition as knowledge, or truth (1992). For Crary, this criterion was the capacity to 'see', and therefore verify, the scientific statement. Critically, photography and the camera as a technology of vision was a manifestation of the new epistemic condition ushered in by the Enlightenment. According to Lynne Warren, the 'presumed objectiv[e]' perspective offered by optic instruments 'came to be seen not merely as drawing techniques, but as microcosms of the Enlightenment world view': a world view which she describes as claiming a 'transcendental 'point of view'' (2006: 1245, 1214). Within this new episteme, what is captured in an image is taken as an autonomous truth: an unquestionable point of view. It is a self-corroborated truth which requires no qualification or secondary referent. In this way, the visible exists in an abstract totality of truth. Indeed, not unlike Foucault with his notion of the medical gaze in the *Birth of the Clinic* (1973), Crary points out how this new episteme privileges visual experience as a means of structuring knowledge and truth, insofar as it constituted a privileged term to which statements of truth and knowledge must conform to in order to be accepted as such. For both Foucault and Crary, the construction of truth and knowledge similarly affected the construction of subjectivity. Foucault saw the subject as being made docile by the gaze; whilst, for Crary, the subject becomes the 'observer', which he defines as a subject who views, and through this viewing, conforms to a particular set of pre-established rules which structure the perceptions and interpretations of the observed object.

In this sense, the observing subject of the photograph, therefore, conforms to the statement of the image. We will discuss the effects on subjectivity further in Chapter 5.

Following on from the camera and photography, and continuing the epistemic order of visibility and objective truth, the next key iteration of "transparency" occurred in reference to glass architecture. The introduction of glass as an architectural material in the 19th century was considered ground-breaking. Paul Scheerbart, the author of *Glasarchitecktur*, spoke of how 'the new glass milieu will transform humanity utterly' (1999: 32). One of the key moments in the history of glass architecture was the construction of The Great Exhibition, of Crystal Palace, a temporary glass structure designed as a space to showcase the manufactured items and technological advances of the world, located in Hyde Park, London, and erected in 1851. The Crystal Palace, 'a building whose most significant property was transparency' (Richards, 1990: 102), stood as a monumental glorification of the ideals of transparency within Victorian modernism, representing the cutting edge of technology, modernism and aesthetics. While the Crystal Palace remains an important symbol for understanding the value of transparency within Victorian architecture specifically and Victorian society more broadly (see Armstrong, 2008), it is in the 20th century that we see a clear correlation between transparency, glass architecture and notions of political openness, particularly in the designs for the building of the League of Nations.

In 1927, an architectural competition was launched to source a design for a building to house the League of Nations in Geneva. This was an entirely novel architectural tender to design a structure to house a pioneering international institution established to ensure world peace and enact global governance. Two notable entries were received. The first from Le Corbusier (together with Pierre Jeanneret), and the second from Hannes Meyer (with Hans Wittwer). While Le Corbusier was already renowned for his use of glass architecture, both modernist architects drew on glass in their entries as a political metaphor for democratic and open governance. Premised on the political purchase of transparent and visible public spaces, Meyer's entry describes a space with,

No pillared reception rooms for weary monarchs, but hygienic work rooms for the busy representatives of their nations. No backrooms for backstairs diplomacy, but open glassed rooms for public negotiations of honest men.

(cited in Frampton, 1982: 143)

Meyer's anaphoric statement constituted one of the first modern uses of transparency as a political metaphor, invoking a way of governance made visible to the public. Yet, in his use of the word 'hygienic' Meyer implies that this kind of political transparency is, as Foucault states in his criticism of Enlightenment rationality, not 'a timeless and essential secret' (1972: 78) that has finally been uncovered, but rather, a deliberately crafted condition, or claim, of modern politics.

Le Corbusier's design and use of glass architecture in his competition entry similarly suggests a tension within the idea of transparency. Authored less than 20 years after the League of Nations architectural competition, Colin Rowe and Robert Slutzky wrote an analysis of Le Corbusier's design for the Palace of the League of Nations in what was to become a much quoted exposition on the use of transparency in glass architecture (1997). For Slutzky and Rowe the value of glass architecture is measured against its abstract aestheticism and fluid borders, demonstrated with effect in the design to the German Bauhaus – a school of art whose architectural design had been famously likened by Sigfried Giedion to cubism. However, they held Le Corbusier's use of glass architecture and transparency for the League of Nation's building design to be ineffective: fixed and domineering, lending nothing to the vision or aesthetics of his design. Together with the critique of Meyer's design, the designs for the Palace of the League of Nations the politics of transparency becomes apparent. Armstrong describes this as 'the imperturbable sheen of glass [which] fails to recognize the importunity of irrational needs, and pathologies dissent' (2008: 163). In this sense, in Meyer and Le Corbusier's designs for the Palace of the League of Nations, transparency becomes an assertive pre-condition of the politics that are to transpire within.

Transparency as metaphor

Where once transparency denoted a literal property of visibility, with the designs for the Palace of the League of Nations, the literal and metaphoric notions of transparency come together. The diachronic rise of transparency from a literal application in architecture to a metaphor for political openness signifies its entrance into discourse. Yet, in the ready appropriation of transparency in modern society today, its metaphorical structure is forgotten, for transparency is not literally applicable. An institution, unlike the lens of a camera or the glass walls of a building, is not a physical object which can be clearly seen, or seen through, but a myriad of immaterial concepts, people and politics which, as such, cannot be physically visible, let alone transparent.

For Balkin, the metaphor of transparency makes assumptions about the nature of the disclosure of information which distorts the way in which this process takes place in practice. Balkin writes:
This metaphor (of transparency) assumes:

(1) That the medium is conceptually separate from the object on the other side
(2) That the process of seeing through the medium does not substantially alter the nature of the object viewed (1998: 394).

Yet in reality, the medium (transparency) is constructed and enacted by the same author of the information-object, who has, in addition, the power to control the form of disclosure, the information disclosed and, arguably, the way in which that information is received. In terms of access to information laws, the State establishes the medium of transparency (the access to information law) to disclose information it also authored. The State additionally bestows itself with the legalised power to decree the form and extent of information disclosed. For access to information laws, this relates to the exemptions from disclosure which, in practice, tend to be over-utilised by the State in favour of non-disclosure. Fenster raises a similar concern when he discusses the paradox between the many ongoing campaigns for freedom of information laws and transparency, and the failure of these laws to achieve real change in terms of good, legitimate governance. He notes too that:

> Once open government laws begin to recognize exceptions to disclosure, the exceptions in turn threaten to unravel the ideal of transparency by vesting broad discretion about whether and how much to disclose in the very state actors that have claimed the exceptions in the first place.
>
> (2017: 11)

Part of this obfuscation of transparency occurs as the metaphorical structure of the concept works, through its linguistic abstraction, to conceal – or make invisible – the way in which information disclosure takes place in practice, concealing specifically the potential power disclosing institutions bear in the process of disclosure.

In addition, Balkin's description of the transparency metaphor as assuming that transparency is 'conceptually separate from the object on the other side' and 'does not substantially alter' that which is disclosed, is central to understanding transparency's claim to neutrality.

Specifically, transparency positions itself as a pure, un-mediating medium through which information travels unscathed. This claim that transparency is a 'pure medium' which does not participate in the representation and interpretation of that which it discloses is bound up with its claim to truth. It is a claim which arises from, or is made possible by, the discursive statements of transparency, such as 'transparency engenders trust', 'transparency is essential for democracy' and 'transparency is a pre-requisite for accountability'. Indeed, these statements both require transparency to be, and construct transparency as, a mechanism for the disclosure of truth, in so far as it is conceived as a neutral carrier of information which does not alter, or prescribe value to, the information it discloses. The narrative of transparency and trust is premised upon transparency delivering 'truth' which can be trusted, as, if not, trust would be misplaced. While, in addition, the conceptual linkages between transparency, democracy and accountability rest upon a fundamental assertion that the information disclosed is 'true', as only if that information is 'true' can it be used to hold governments to account and effectively participate in policy reform.

Transparency's claim to truth also arises from its metaphorical association of 'making visible', which, as we have traced here, arise from its literal history. Note Adrian Henriques' definition of transparency in his book *Corporate Truth: The Limits to Transparency*:

> Transparency means conveying the truth. The origin of the word is to carry something across. What should be carried across is the truth. So transparency means seeing clearly.
>
> It is ironic that the word 'transparency' seems itself to be both rather hard to define and to have two apparently different meanings. On hearing the word, usually the first thing we think of is glass; glass is transparent because light passes through it and so you can see what is behind. But there is also another meaning, such as when we say that someone behaved transparently – in other words you can see that they were up to. In this case the light is reflected by the behaviour, making it visible. As a result, there is no agenda, nothing hidden.
>
> (2007: 30, italics in original)

Henriques' reasoning for transparency as the conveyer of truth recalls transparency's ocularcentric history in photography and glass architecture. For Henrique, transparency 'means conveying the truth' because 'transparency means seeing clearly': truth and sight are equivalent, what is 'visible' and clearly seen is necessarily 'true'. Thus, to make visible means to make true, both because that which is seen is 'true' and because the process of making visible – transparency – is itself a 'pure medium' that does not alter the 'truth' of what it brings into visibility. It is 'true' because 'there is no agenda', because as a visibility it is considered neutral and value-free: there is 'nothing hidden' and nothing else to it. This is just as Ana Acosta describes in her critique of the imposition of transparency upon the female body in Sarah Scott's *Millennium Hall* and Marquis de Sade's *120 Days of Sodom*: 'the discursive transparency is constructed through the unambiguous conceit that the narrative explains thoroughly and completely, for everyone, everything there is to understand' (2007: 113). This is an integral aspect of the transparency narrative which works to problematise privacy, secrecy and the private space, discussed in more detail in Chapter 5 of this book.

This critical claim to neutrality is echoed within practices of transparency where the information disclosed is itself considered value-free and neutral. A good example of this is open data and with it, e-government, are considered the 'new frontier' (Sunlight Foundation, 2014: 18) of transparency, and fervently advocated by the Open Government Partnership (see also Chapter 3). As Clare Birchall puts it, '[e]-transparency [...] is seen to deliver 'original' data and information free from human distortion and the attendant 'risks' of re-presentation' (2014: 87). It is a claim that, as Birchall notes, the transparency narrative rests upon: '[t]his vision of the pure medium [transparency] delivering raw, self-evident, neutral data is inherent to the advocacy of e-transparency' (2014: 90).[1] Indeed, open data makes a compelling claim to being a 'pure medium' insofar as it seems to come from nowhere, without immediately discernible authorship or mediating agencies. Data are broadly presented as objective: rational, value-free measurements, subject only to prescribed controls and formulaic permutations. This neutralised presentation of data means it is taken as pre-discursive and, as Kitchen notes, 'free of political ideology' (2014: 3). Yet, as Gupta rightly points out, 'information (including scientific information) is neither value-neutral nor universally valid' (2008: 5), but is instead always already situated within a particular context which it both produces and is produced by: information and data are always already discursive.

This analysis raises questions such as what acts of representation and interpretation are involved in transparency, and at what stage in the allegory of transparency do such acts occurs? What does this mean for the political validity of the information it discloses? And what does this mean for the institutions which author the information and instigate the process of transparency? Indeed, in answering these questions, disclosure brought about through mechanisms of transparency must be understood as a form of interpretation and therefore, necessarily, must also be understood as altering that which is disclosed. But disclosure, as an act of interpretation, must also be understood as occurring within a chain of interpretation and value-inscription as information, too, is not neutral or pre-interpretive. It is always already an interpretation.

Summary

This chapter has traced a brief history of the concept of transparency. I have mapped the historical and diachronic transformation of transparency from a literal application (in photography and architecture) to a rhetorical device (a metaphor), which signals its entrance into discourse. As I have shown, transparency is positioned as an Enlightenment value, and subsequently as an international human right in the form of the right of access to information. With its historic connection to the Enlightenment, transparency becomes bracketed, together with rights discourse and other narratives of freedom, as an *a priori*, neutral and unquestionable value that betters the historical place of humankind. In part through its later metaphorical construction, transparency continues to reassert its neutrality as a pure, un-mediating, medium, that does not alter – or ascribe any political or ideological value – to the information it reveals. I have discussed here how this claim is bound up with its claim to truth, upon which discursive statements such as "transparency brings about accountability", or "transparency fosters trust", rests. Indeed, we have explored here how, constructed as an un-mediating medium, transparency conceals its agency in the processes of representation and interpretation inherent in the disclosure, transfer or communication of information, instead positing information as true, neutral and pre-interpretive.

In the next chapters, I continue to trace the historical evolution of the discourse of transparency and particularly its manifestation in national access to information laws (Chapter 2) and in global governance (Chapter 3).

Note

1 For Birchall, it is in this way (through its apparent neutrality) that transparency claims superiority over other forms of narrative disclosure, including gossip, scandal and conspiracy theory (2014).

Further reading

Acosta, A. M. 2007. Transparency and the Enlightenment Body: Utopian Space in Sarah Scott's Millenium Hall and Sade's The 120 Days of Sodom. In N. Pohl & B. Tooley (eds). *Gender and Utopia in the Eighteenth Century: Essays in English and French Utopia Writing.* London: Routledge, pp. 117–120.

Adams, R., & Adeleke, F. 2019. Media and the Right of Access to Information in Africa. In A. Adekunle. (ed). *Freedom of Information and Democratic Governance in Nigeria.* Lagos: NIALS Publication, pp. 11–25.

Armstrong, I. 2008. *Victorian Glassworlds: Glass Culture and the Imagination 1830–1880.* Oxford: Oxford University Press.

Balkin, J. M. 1998. How Mass Media Simulate Political Transparency. *Cultural Values* 3(4): 393–413.

Birchall, C. 2014. Radical Transparency? *Cultural Studies – Critical Methodologies* 14(1): 77–88.

Björkstrand, G., & Mustonen, J. 2006. Introduction. In J. Mustonen. (ed). *The World's First Freedom of Information Act.* Kokkola: Anders Chydenius Foundation, pp. 4–7.

Blanton, T. S. 2006. 240 Years After the First Freedom of Information Law, Access to Government Information Now Seen as a Human Right. In J. Mustonen (ed). *The World's First Freedom of Information Act. Anders Chydenius' Legacy Today.* Kokkola: Anders Chydenius, pp. 80–97.

Case of *Claude Reyes et al v Chile*, Claude Reyes and ors v Chile, Merits, reparations and costs, IACHR Series C no 151, IHRL 1535 (IACHR 2006), 19th September 2006, Inter-American Court of Human Rights.

Crary, J. 1992. *Techniques of the Observer: On Vision and Modernity in the Nineteenth Century.* Massachusetts: October Books.

Fenster, M. 2017. *The Transparency Fix: Secrets, Leaks and Uncontrollable Government Information.* Stanford, CA: Stanford University Press.

Florini, A. M. 1999. Does the Invisible Hand Require a Transparent Glove: The Politics of Transparency. Paper prepared for the Annual World Bank Conference on Development Economies, Washington, D.C., 28–30 April 1999.

Foucault, M. 1971. Nietzsche, Genealogy, History. In P. Rabinow (ed). *The Foucault Reader.* New York: Pantheon Books, pp. 76–100.

Foucault, M. 1972[1969]. *Archaeology of Knowledge and the Discourse on Language* Trans. A. M. Sheridan Smith. New York: Pantheon Books.

Foucault, M. 1973. *The Birth of the Clinic.* Trans. A. Sheridan. New York: Pantheon Books.

Frampton, K. 1982. *Modern Architecture: A Critical History.* London: Thames and Hudson.

Geroulanos, S. 2017. *Transparency in Postwar France: A Critical History of the Present.* Stanford, CA: Stanford University Press.

Giedion, S. 1982. *Space, Time and Architecture: The Growth of a New Tradition.* 5th Edition. Cambridge, MA: Harvard University Press.

Gupta, A. 2008. Transparency Under Scrutiny: Information Disclosure in Global Environmental Governance. *Global Environmental Politics* 8(2): 1–7.

Hansen, H. K., Christensen, L. T., & Flyverbom, M. 2015. Introduction: Logics of Transparency in Late Modernity: Paradoxes, Mediation and Governance. *European Journal of Social Theory* 18(2): 117–131.

Hood, C., & Heald, D. (eds). 2006. *Transparency: The Key to Better Governance?* Oxford: Oxford University Press.

International Monetary Fund, Working Group. 1998. Report of the Working Group on Transparency and Accountability. Washington: International Monetary Fund. Available from: www.imf.org/external/np/g22/taarep.pdf [Accessed 10 August 2019].

Kitchen, R. 2014. The Real-Time City? Big Data and Smart Urbanism. *Geo-Journal* 79(1): 1–14.

Levitt, T. 2009. *The Shadow of Enlightenment: Optical and Political Transparency in France 1789–1848*. Oxford: Oxford University Press.

Meijer, A. 2013. The History of Transparency: Analyzing the Long-term Socio-Political Construction of Transparency in the Netherlands. Paper prepared for the International Conference on Transparency Research, Paris, October 24th–26th 2013.

Richards, T. 1990. *The Commodity Culture of Victorian England: Advertising and the Spectacle, 1851–1914*. Stanford, CA: Stanford University Press.

Rowe, C., & Slutzky, R. 1997. *Transparency*. Basel: Birkhäuser Architecture.

Scheerbart, P., & Taut, B. 1914. *Glasarchitecktur*. Quoted in W. Benjamin. 1991. *Selected Writings Volume 2 1927–1934*. Trans. R. Livingstone & Others. Cambridge, MA: Belknap Press.

Sunlight Foundation. 2014. Quoted in City of Oakland, Public Ethics Commission. Toward Collaborative Transparency. Available from: www2.oaklandnet.com/w/oak044713. [Accessed 10 August 2019].

Vidler, A. 2005. Transparency and Utopia: Constructing the Void from Pascal to Foucault. In M. Marrinan & J. Bender (eds). *Regimes of Description: In the Archive of the Eighteenth Century*. Stanford, CA: Stanford University Press, pp. 175–198.

Warren, L. 2006. *Encyclopaedia of Twentieth-Century Photography*. New York: Routledge.

2 Access to information delimited

Introduction

> How unpleasant it is to reveal the limitations and necessities of a practice where one is used to seeing, in all its pure transparency, the expression of genius and freedom
>
> (Foucault, 1972: 210)

In 2000, the then South African president signed into law the Promotion of Access to Information Act (PAIA). The passing of this Act into law marked the first access to information (ATI) law on the African continent, and took place at a historical moment when countries across the world, and particularly in Europe, were adopting similar laws. According to a survey in 2018 by leading ATI scholar, David Banisar, almost 120 countries have now enacted a comprehensive national ATI law. Another six countries have a national policy or regulation relating to ATI. And a further 30 countries have begun processes for developing an ATI law, the vast majority of which are countries from the African region (Banisar, 2018). Thus, ATI laws are now prevalent in most countries across the globe, providing legislated means – in the form of a rights claim – for citizens to gain access to government information and providing governments with the means to advance a claim to transparency on its subjects.

Yet, as this chapter will explore, these laws arise from a particular world view and way of thinking which can work to exclude those who do not participate in its terms. Accordingly, analysed here is the way in which ATI laws delimit other realities, ways of governing and kinds of information or knowledge which cannot be reduced to a disclosable "record". I refer here to the notion of 'epistemic violence' developed by Gayatri Chakravorty Spivak to name the way in which subaltern knowledges – and indeed subjectivities (on this see particularly Chapter 5) – are rewritten by privileged Western knowledge and knowledge systems. In making these arguments, I draw on the South African PAIA as an example.

Epistemic violence of transparency

In her seminal essay, 'Can the Subaltern Speak?', Spivak draws on Foucault's concept of discourse to understand the epistemic process through which the imperialists constitute the colonial 'other' as a discursive 'subject', and colonial knowledges and knowledge systems as inferior to those of the West (1993). She names this process 'epistemic violence'. (Within this context and following Foucaultian thought, epistemic can be broadly understood as relating to the assemblage of rules that govern the structure of discourse and knowledge within a particular historic period.) In part, the subjugation of the colonial 'other' takes place through the recording and documenting of the colonial subject by the imperialist. This creation of knowledge and too, archives, on the colonial subject both rewrites and marginalises the colonial subject's own epistemic traditions. Citing from Foucault, Spivak writes,

> Perhaps it is no more than to ask that the subtext of the palimpsestic narrative of imperialism be recognized as "subjugated knowledge", "a whole set of knowledges that have been disqualified as inadequate to their task or insufficiently elaborated: naive knowledges, located low down on the hierarchy, beneath the required level of cognition or scientificity".
>
> (1993: 76)

In this way, the epistemic values of the colonial subject/other are occluded from what is formally recognised and recorded as historical truth. The subject is *spoken for* by colonialist regimes of truth and knowledge. It is for this reason that Spivak questions whether the subaltern can speak, ultimately suggesting that he/she cannot.

With regard to transparency, as it is heralded as a premium value of the modern and developed world, what takes place is the marginalisation and exclusion of other means of governance, other forms of information and knowledge, and indeed an exclusion of individuals and communities who do not ascribe to the same ideals. One of the ways in which this takes place is through access to information laws.

Law and exclusion

In its preamble, PAIA delineates that one of the key objectives of the Act is to 'foster a culture of transparency' (2000). Considered a model access to information law, the Act places an obligation on both public and private bodies to respond to access to information requests which follow the prescribed procedure. It further details a series of categories of information which are exempted from disclosure: some discretional and some mandatory. However, the Act – like many other freedom of information laws – puts in place procedures for accessing records of public and private bodies which are onerous, bureaucratic and legalistic. Requesters must first decide whether the record they are seeking access to is held by a public or private body (often not such an obvious distinction to decipher), before filling out a Form A (to a public body) or a Form B (to a private body). These forms require the requester to provide various personal details, and to pay an access fee. If a public body refuses access, or simply fails to respond to the access to information request, the requester has a 60-day period in which to lodge an appeal (using Form C). If the request to a private body was unsuccessful for whatever reason, the only recourse is to the courts. Ordinary citizens are required to follow these complex procedures before an access to information request can even be considered,[1] which effectively means PAIA is structurally inaccessible to those outside the knowledge, chain or structure of bureaucracy, as will be discussed further below.

In the South African context, access to information is considered a fundamental human right, which is provided for within the Bill of Rights of the Constitution. Yet, by creating such a complex and bureaucratic process for the exercise of this right, PAIA reasserts the power and legitimacy of the state as both the legitimate holder of records, and a legitimate state insofar as it can boast an ATI law that provides for access to records. (We will discuss further in Chapter 3 about the global status afforded to countries with access to information laws.) Indeed, the language of the Act arguably makes this clear: citizens, or "requesters" are only allowed "access" to records upon formal "request". The fact that in most cases (and not just in South Africa) the request is simply denied or ignored, repeats this assertion of the power of state and its legitimacy as the holder of records. In these circumstances, the practice of ATI laws appears a far mark away from the broad narrative of access to information that '[g]overnments collect and hold information on behalf of people' (Open Government Partnership, 2011).

The way in which access to information laws work to exclude and delimit other realities is also evident in the kind of states and systems of government they necessitate. As Garsten and de Montoya have pointed out, transparency is considered 'central for the making of the modern state' (2008: 2). Indeed, a state which boasts an access to information law and which ranks low in Transparency International's Corruption Barometer is considered advanced, modern and democratic. Conversely, however, in creating the image of what an ideal state should look like, those states that do not conform or match this image, are rendered lagging, behind and undemocratic.

Darch and Underwood have argued that one of the key elements necessary for a state to claim transparency and enjoy the reputation of modern statehood, is a bureaucratic and centralised administration. They note particularly that 'freedom of information is meaningless outside the framework of the modern bureaucratic State' (2010: 95), which has been described in brief above. In short, ATI laws require a centralised State based on the rule of law, with formal compliance and record keeping systems. This is notable in ATI laws not only in terms of record keeping and compliance provisions, but also the internal review process (only provided which respect to an access request made to a public body, as mentioned above). In an internal review, a more senior official conducts a secondary review of the decision made on an access to information request, and therefore necessitating a formal hierarchical structure of institutional administration.

Not all countries around the globe, however, enjoy a bureaucratic State or centralised system of governance. Within the African content many States consist of a plethora of different and distinct linguistic and cultural communities within one formal polity, forming a largely pluralist form of governance. This designation of 'pluralist' does not accord with the 'structural pluralism' spoken of by Giddens in relation to the increasing role and relevance of the private sector in the governance of Africa (2000: 55), nor is it in relation to the political pluralism created through the various engaged actors of democracy.[2] The pluralism which is evident in a number of African countries relates to the various governing systems, including, but not limited to, the modern centralised government who enacts power through formal laws and policies, as well as the traditional systems of power and rule which perform their functions in smaller communities and spaces based on culturally accepted values and norms (Ntsebeza, 2004; Ferguson, 2006; Santos, 2006; Clarke, 2009). However, the transparency discourse works to declare these kinds of systems of governance, where the formal rule of law is not universal, such as in pluralist systems of governance, as illegitimate and undemocratic.

In South Africa, for example, the formal system of law necessary for a bureaucratic State is not recognised by, or accessible to, all those living in the country. This came to the fore with the passage of the Traditional Courts Bill,[3] which was drafted to bring the traditional customary law – which operates across most of the rural and some the urban areas of South Africa – under central and formal rule of law. One of the major arguments for the formal recognition of traditional customary law is that many South Africans are simply unable to access formal law, whether on account of expense, location or that it represents different cultural values which certain groups do not necessary accept. With regard to PAIA, in cases where the access to information request has been denied or ignored, the only recourse is through the courts. Yet, as a complex and costly process requiring not only access to the formal system of justice, but also legal capacity, this is simply inaccessible to so many living in South Africa. According to Kathleen Janssen, this is a broad problematic of these kinds of laws. She states that 'access legislation [...] only benefits the small part of the public that is already equipped with sufficient knowledge about governmental processes and ways to participate in them' (2012: 4–5). It is interesting to note that a similar argument has been lodged against the concept of open data, whose benefits can only be reaped by those with the knowledge, skills and capacity to understand and process complex datasets (Adams & Adeleke, 2016).

Similar to the way in which access to information laws delimit other forms of governance, access to information laws also work to override other understandings of knowledge, and particularly, 'information'. Although PAIA enables 'the right of access to information' as guaranteed under section 32 of the South African Constitution, it provides only for access to 'records'. Records are defined under the Act as 'any recorded information regardless of form or medium'. In translating the right of access to 'information' of the constitution into the right of access to 'records' in PAIA, the scope of the constitutional right to information was limited. Judge Cameron J, in his minority judgement in the matter handed down between *My Vote Counts NPC v Speaker of the National Assembly and Others* in the South African Constitutional Court in 2015, has commented on this specific issue. For Cameron J,

> PAIA affords a right of access to 'records'. It does not define 'information'. It contains only a definition of 'record'. This limits the operation of the statute to information that is recorded in some form or medium. Oral communications containing or constituting information are excluded. Also not contemplated are situations

that may require physical access to a place in order to obtain information that is yet to be reduced to material form, such as a meeting of a parliamentary portfolio committee, a court hearing or inspecting the site of past happenings. Are these omissions serious? It would appear so. Depending on the nature of the information, and the possible disincentives to preserving it, the absence of an encompassing definition, underscores PAIA's limited ambit. This is because a contract, undertaking, understanding, agreement or donation may all be orally concluded. In that event, as far as PAIA is concerned, there is no 'record' – and hence no right of access to that information. This limited ambit creates obvious risks that some deal–doers will want to keep their transactions spoken, so that they are not 'recorded'.

(Para 97–98)[4]

Cameron's point is certainly important. However, the limitation of PAIA to 'records' also excludes other kinds of information and knowledge that may not be formally recorded, nor ascribes to the Western model of knowledge as scriptocentric.

Darch and Underwood have discussed this point in relation to the privileging of documents and records that has occurred as a result of the institutionalisation (and formalisation) of information, of which access to information laws are a part. The authors write:

The 'information rich/information poor' debate has been characterised largely in terms of *access to documents*, be they in electronic, print–on–paper, or other *recorded* forms. What has been ignored is the information culture to be found in any community, which comprises a mixture of oral and recorded knowledge and perceptions. We should remember that for a substantial time, the only reason for recording something was because it was considered *not worth memorising.*

(2002: 33, italics as in original)

While Darch and Underwood raise an interesting idea about recorded information pertaining to that which was 'not worth memorising', their analysis also reveals the workings of the transparency discourse. For, what is taking place is the demarcation of the boundaries of the signification of 'knowledge' and 'information' such that these other forms of knowledge and information spoken of by Darch and Underwood are excluded from the site of meaning in a manifest example of epistemic violence: they are rendered non-information and non-knowledge.

For Carol Smart – who draws on post-structuralist thought within her feminist critique of law – exclusion and self-legitimisation are law's very essence (1996). Indeed, she argues that the very purpose of law is to reassert the power of the State. Addressing what she speaks of as the limitations of Foucault's theories to adequately focus on the oppressive power of law, Smart asserts that law, as a system of knowledge, places itself above other forms of knowledge. Law, she states, 'sets itself outside the social order, as if through the application of legal method and rigour it becomes a thing apart which can in turn reflect upon the world from which it is divorced' (1996: 428). Smart goes on to argue that 'the more it [the law] is seen as a unified discipline that responds only to its own coherent, internal logic, the more powerful it becomes' (1996: 428). Golder and Fitzpatrick, who have responded to the critique of Foucault's limited appraisal of law as a structure of power, set out a different understanding to Smart of the way in which law works with forces of power. They speak of law not as a 'unified' and self-contained discipline, but rather a 'self-resistant, responsive' force that 'must necessarily exceed itself if it is to remain law' (2009: 82). It is in this way that Golder and Fitzpatrick describe law as illimitable. Indeed, for Golder and Fitzpatrick, Foucault's law cannot correspond to that described by Smart, to a law that 'responds only to its own [...] logic', as, they argue, 'for law incipiently to be other to its present instantiation, it cannot be definitively tied to any singular and determinate force' (2009: 83), especially a force which is – as Smart suggests – its own. It is, instead, it's very 'vacuity' from which law gains its power. Thus, concurring with Golder and Fitzpatrick I suggest that it is *through* law, and not (as Smart might argue) *because of* law, that transparency, and the power of the state as the holder of information and knowledge, becomes legitimated. This is supported by the fact that the discourse of transparency has exceeded far beyond the limits of access to information laws.

In its continual re-affirmation of its value and legitimacy through access to information laws and other structures of transparency (discussed in the following chapters) the discourse of transparency reproduces itself. But as claims to transparency work to legitimise the forces of power which author them, they also render that which does not adopt the rhetoric of transparency as illegitimate, as outside of discourse. It is in this way that discourse operates in a way that is fundamentally – and intrinsically – exclusionary.

Summary

This chapter has explored the ways in which access to information laws work to exclude and delimit other realities, and particularly other forms of governance that are not centralised and bureaucratic, and other forms of knowledge or information that cannot be contained within a disclosable record.

Yet, access to information laws have become one small aspect of the larger discourse on transparency which encompasses broad commitments to transparency on a global and policy level. This is the focus of the following chapter. In addition, in Chapter 5 I examine the crisis of access to information laws posed by complex AI-driven technologies which go well beyond the "record/disclosure" paradigm that these laws set out.

Notes

1 By way of comparison, under the Nigerian Freedom of Information Act, 2011, a request for information held by a government body can be requested in writing, through a third party or orally. This is rare provision of access to information laws globally.
2 See, for example, Owusu (1997) for a discussion on the democratic pluralism and the African state.
3 Note that this Bill has currently been withdrawn from Parliament, although their remains broad commitment to bringing the traditional system of law under the auspices of the formal system.
4 Cameron's verdict was handed down on a matter regarding whether PAIA adequately enabled the right of access to information, according to section 32(2), noting that it did not place an obligation on political parties to disclose its sources of private funding. Cameron notes a point about the definition of records which prevents the creation of records. Whilst the South African PAIA does not place an obligation upon information holders to create records, the Model Law on Access to Information for Africa of the African Commission on Human and Peoples' Rights, addresses this shortfall by including a provision of this nature. The Model Law on Access to Information for Africa of the African Commission on Human and Peoples' Rights (2013) provides for the duty to create, keep and maintain records under Section 6.

Further reading

Ackerman, J. M. 2006. The Global Explosion of Freedom of Information Laws. *Administrative Law Review* 58(1): 85–130.
Adams, R., & Adeleke, F. 2016. Assessing the Potential Role of Open Data in South African Environmental Management. *The African Journal of Information and Communication* 19(1): 79–99.

Banisar, D. 2018. National Right to Information Laws, Regulations and Initiatives 2018. Available from: doi:10.2139/ssrn.1857498. [Accessed 13 August 2019].

Clarke, K. M. 2009. *Fictions of Justice: The International Criminal Court and the Challenge of Legal Pluralism in Sub-Saharan Africa*. Cambridge: Cambridge University Press.

Constitutional Court of South Africa. 2015. *My Vote Counts NPC v Speaker of the National Assembly and Others* CCT 121/14.

Darch, C., & Underwood, P. G. 2002. Information Literacy in Africa: Empowerment or Impoverishment. *ACAS Bulletin* No. 62/63: 30–34.

Darch, C., & Underwood, P. G. 2010. *Freedom of Information and the Developing World: The Citizen, the State and Models of Openness*. Oxford: Chandos Publishing.

Ferguson, J. 2006. *Global Shadows: Africa in the Neoliberal World Order*. Durham, NC and London: Duke University Press.

Foucault, M. 1972. *Archaeology of Knowledge and the Discourse on Language*. Trans. A. M. Sheridan Smith. New York: Pantheon Books.

Foucault, M. 1989. *The Order of Things*. London: Routledge.

Garsten, C., & de Montoya, M. L. (eds). 2008. *Transparency in a New Global Order: Unveiling Organizational Visions*. Cheltenham: Edward Elgar Publishing.

Giddens, A. 2000. *The Third Way and its Critics*. Oxford: Polity Press.

Golder, B., & Fitzpatrick, P. 2009. *Foucault's Law*. Abingdon: Routledge.

Hazell, R., Worthy, B., & Glover, M. 2010. *The Impact of the Freedom of Information Act on Central Government in the UK – Does FOI Work?* London: Palgrave.

Janssen, K. 2012. Open Government Data and the Right to Information: Opportunities and Obstacles. *The Journal of Community Informatics* 8(2): n.pag.

Klaaren, J. 2014. The Cost of Justice. Briefing Paper for Public Positions Theme Event, 24 March 2014, WiSER, History Workshop and Wits Political Studies Department. Available from: http://wiser.wits.ac.za/system/files/documents/Klaaren%20-%20Cost%20of%20Justice%20-%20%202014.pdf. [Accessed 13 August 2019].

Ntsebeza, L. 2004. Democratic Decentralization and Traditional Authority: Dilemmas of Land Administration in Rural South Africa. *European Journal of Development Research* 16(1): 71–89.

Open Government Partnership. 2011. Open Government Partnership Declaration. Available from: www.ogp.gov.za/?q=node/17. [Accessed 13 August 2019].

Osuwu, M. 1997. Domesticating Democracy: Culture, Civil Society and Constitutionalism in Africa. *Comparative Studies in Society and History* 39(1): 120–152.

Republic of South Africa. 1996. Constitution of the Republic of South Africa, Act 108 of 1996.

Republic of South Africa. 2000. Promotion of Access to Information, Act, 2 of 2000.

Santos, B. S. 2006. The Heterogeneous State and Legal Pluralism in Mozambique. *Law & Society Review* 40(1): 39–76.

Smart, C. 1996. The Power of Law. In J. Muncie et al. (eds). *Criminological Perspectives: A Reader.* London: Thousand Oaks, pp. 423–431.

Spivak, G. C. 1993. Can the Subaltern Speak? In L. Chrisman & P. Williams. (eds). *Colonial Discourse and Post-Colonial Theory: A Reader.* Hemel Hempstead: Harvester, pp. 66–111.

3   Transparency universal

Introduction

> I believe in Transparency
>
> (Clinton, 2012)

Transparency works globally on two levels. First, as a principle of global governance, espoused through frameworks including the Rule of Transparency in Treaty-Based Investor State Arbitration of the United Nations (UN) Commission on International Trade Law (2014) and the UN Economic Commission for Europe (UNECE) Convention on Access to Information, Public Participation in Decision-Making and Access to Justice in Environmental Matters (Aarhus Convention, 1998) (Bianchi & Peters, 2013). Second, given its global status and the way in which global governance regimes inspect and measure domestic laws, policies and practices, transparency is also reworking and restructuring the organisation of global society. It celebrates those parts of the world where transparency claims reverberate as progressive, modern, and enlightened, and it chastises 'developing' states where transparency remains unseen and unclaimed as 'lagging behind'. At best, these states are being guided (by international actors) on an inevitable path towards greater transparency through the enactment of internationally set standards on openness and information disclosure which claim, above all, a consensual universality. The idea, then, has become an important tool for organising global society; not just in organising the distinction between the developed and developing world, but also in organising the image of what the 'developed' world looks like, and conversely what the 'developing world' should look like. In this, I rely on Jacques Lacan's understanding of discourse as entailing and shaping social relations in so far as it entails and shapes linguistic, symbolic relations (2007). It is as such that discourse implies what

Foucault has called 'the problem of power' (1980: 212), which I explore here in terms of the ethics of transparency and its imaginative content in modern society.

Continuing the discussion from the previous chapter on Spivak's notion of epistemic violence, I consider here how this particular framework clears a space for a new understanding of the recent global movement of transparency within a neo-imperialist context. Moreover, by recognising the global spread of transparency as epistemic violence, it allows us to more fully understand the ways in which the transparency discourse marginalises other forms of governance, and other historical truths, as discussed in detail in the previous chapter.

Transparency and inclusivity

Following the dearth of access to information laws in the early 2000s, in 2011 the Open Government Partnership (OGP) was founded with the aim of universalising transparency through the establishment of a global network of transparency champions. However, only eligible countries can join the OGP. Eligibility is dependent on the domestic commitments made by interested countries on the four key areas set out by the OGP: fiscal transparency, access to information, asset disclosure and citizen engagement. Currently, 79 countries are members of the OGP. Twelve of these countries are sub-Saharan African.

On joining the OGP member states must endorse the Open Government Declaration which, in short, sets out the OGPs ideology on transparency and openness and provides one of the most high-level overviews of how the meaning and value of transparency is conceived at a global level. Critically, transparency is a value that the OGP insists is both universal and inclusive. Note the opening statement of the Declaration:

> We acknowledge that people all around the world are demanding more openness in government. They are calling for greater civic participation in public affairs, and seeking ways to make their governments more transparent, responsive, accountable, and effective.
>
> We recognize that countries are at different stages in their efforts to promote openness in government, and that each of us pursues an approach consistent with our national priorities and circumstances and the aspirations of our citizens.
>
> (2011)

As a discourse which claims inclusivity and universality, all are required to participate in transparency's arrangements. Transparency, it seems, speaks for everyone. The declarative statement made in this Declaration that 'people all around the world are demanding more openness in government' holds an implicit discursive power. It embeds the claim that the global project of transparency is both geographically and ideologically neutral, being 'demand[ed]' equally 'all around the world'. Moreover, the power of global and State institutions in authoring the transparency discourse is refuted in the grammatical insistence of this statement: transparency is being demanded by the 'people'. The Declaration further negates the possibility of any other kind of governance in stating that 'countries are at different stages in their efforts to promote openness in government', as if open government is a singular inevitability that all countries everywhere are working towards fulfilling.

The tag-line of the opposition party in South Africa makes a similar, perhaps unintended, conceit in its proclamation of an 'Open opportunity society for all'. The isocolon draws a parallel between the words 'open' and 'all', equating an open society as necessarily inclusive and one in which 'all' can, if not must, participate. But, as Tero Erkkila points out, the inclusivity of transparency and openness marks a constraint:

> Openness is seen as a mechanism for political inclusion, but nevertheless it marks constraints and a new focusing on the responsibilities of the government, while the citizens, interest groups and market actors are seen as having more responsibilities.
>
> (2010: 368)

While for Erkkila the inclusivity of transparency marks a constraint in terms of a re-shuffling of political responsibilities, it also has a hegemonic purchase, leaving no one outside the reach of transparency.

The Declaration goes on to declare that:

> We embrace principles of transparency and open government with a view toward achieving greater prosperity, well–being and human dignity in our own countries and in an increasingly interconnected world.
>
> (OGP, 2011)

The transparency ideology promoted by the OGP is a powerful one, resting upon the language of human rights and freedoms, promising the overall betterment of humankind, and echoing the given history of transparency as emanating out of Enlightenment ideals of freedom and humanity discussed in Chapter 1. Indeed, the opening line of the Declaration asserts this propinquity to human rights: 'As members of the Open Government Partnership, committed to the principles enshrined in the Universal Declaration of Human Rights, the UN Convention against Corruption, and other applicable international instruments related to human rights and good governance' (2011). The transparency claims of the OGP are inherently problematic, as they cannot avoid the significant risk that, without more, they are doomed to remain only abstract rhetoric enunciating the ostensible human benefits of a globalised and transparent world society, and failing to take account of the growing exclusion and oppression of certain groups and ideas in this monolithic endeavours.

It is statements such as those from the OGP that led Clare Birchall to assert that we consider transparency a 'virtue' in modern society (2011: 2), that is, a practice that supposedly cultivates a moral disposition. In a less critical way, Matteo Turilli and Luciano Floridi also attest that transparency holds an ethical content, bringing about countless societal benefits (2010). Yet, what is created by taking transparency as a virtue and its ethical value as *a priori* is both that the concept itself is rendered beyond critique, and that those who do not accept and adopt it are instinctively categorised as immoral, unethical and even (with transparency's claim to human rights) inhumane. Lessig's assertion of 'who can be against transparency? Its virtues are so crushingly obvious' is again pertinent here (2009: 1). It is also through this 'ethics of transparency' that a general fear is cultivated around the idea of the 'hidden' and the 'unseen', as will be discussed further in Chapter 5. Its claim to inclusivity therefore becomes a technique of power by working to create and enforce a hegemonic totality out of which there is no escape considered legitimate.

What is more, through the discourse that speaks of transparency as inclusive, universal and an ethical virtue, an idealised image is projected, and transparency becomes mythologised. For Roland Barthes – one of the key thinkers on myths and mythologisation – mythologisation consists in the perfecting of speech such that it appears both innocent and natural, and even eternal – that is, without any distinct history or origin (1972). The object of myth becomes at once 'naturalized' as fundamental and intrinsic: a self-evident truth. So, when Hilary Clinton proclaimed during the Senate Hearing on the 2012 Benghazi Consulate attack, 'I believe in transparency', she was mythologising transparency, claiming it for a perfect truth. Her sentiments are echoed by John Roberts in his assessment of transparency, and how the discourse of transparency continues to reproduce itself: '[w]e seem to believe in transparency, and with every failure of governance, we have been prone to invest in yet further transparency as the assumed remedy for all failures' (2009: 957–958).

Through these discursive claims that constitute transparency as an inclusive, universal and ethical value, transparency amasses the power to shape not only global relations, but also realities and subjectivities. Foucault speaks of this as the power of discourse to 'systematically form the objects of which it speaks' (1972: 49). Consider, too, Graham Ward's description of the how myth making shapes our material reality:

> What is imagined is subsequently fashioned; the invisibility of thought becomes material culture. What might begin in an 'idolatry of words' may become mausoleums of national heroes (the Panthéon), monuments to democratic ideals (the Lincoln Memorial in Washington), and sites for the veneration of monarchs (the Banqueting House in Whitehall Palace). It is through this generation of symbolic form that belief in myths can foster an immersive and environmental appeal: to an imagined glory, an imagined heroism or martyrdom, and an imagined sociality. [...] the power of such mythic thinking, when culturally pervasive, 'cannot be refuted by syllogisms'. Politically, the only way a myth is overturned is by a revolution, not a reformation. A revolution is a total reimagining of a social and cultural landscape.
>
> (2014: 168)

When Hillary Clinton articulated transparency as a fundamental and transcendental truth to be believed in, she was, no doubt, relying on its mythical status, with the same imagination that erected the Temple to Transparency that I spoke of in the opening of this book. But as Ward suggests, this imagined reality is politically hegemonic. Resistance to it implies allegiance to revolution, and a complete reversal of the symbolic order.

Proselytising transparency

Spivak's notion of epistemic violence (1993), discussed in the previous chapter, is particularly relevant for the examination here on the global and arguably hegemonic spread of the transparency discourse. It is relevant on two accounts. On the one hand, it clears a space for a new understanding of the recent global movement of transparency within a neo-imperialist context, where the values of the West are imposed – or proselytised – on the rest of the world. This will be discussed in further detail below. On the other hand, by recognising the global spread of transparency as epistemic violence, it allows us to consider the ways in which the transparency discourse marginalises[1] other forms of governance, and other historical truths, as discussed in the previous chapter. My concern, therefore, is that the transparency discourse speaks on behalf of the world, and that this 'speaking for' comes distinctly out of the West. Indeed, the unquestioned global appraisal of transparency has made the concept hegemonic.[2] It has become a global standard of statehood and democracy, meaning that those States which do not ascribe to its rhetoric are considered undemocratic, or worse. Such States are excluded from public global forums, such as the OGP, or are regarded sceptically. But it is a standard that largely arose in the West and was later adopted on an international platform, before spreading globally; thus, begging the question as to whether the West (or Western values) still retains a hegemonic control over the production of this discourse.

The proselytisation of transparency across the African region, in particular, can be examined in relation to the OGP and the criteria for membership, of which one of the most important is a national access to information law. Within the African region, since the OGP began in 2011, a significant proliferation of countries have adopted, or are formally deliberating the adoption of, access to information laws, arguably in the hope of joining the ranks of the OGP's transparent elite. Prior to 2011, only four African countries had access to information laws. Those countries were South Africa, Zimbabwe (whose access to information law in effect reduced citizen access to information (Ngwenya, 2018)), Uganda and Angola. Since 2011, 21 more countries have adopted or are considering adopting, access to information laws. These countries are Angola, Benin, Burkino Faso, Côte D'Ivoire; Ethiopia, Ghana; Guinea, Kenya, Liberia, Malawi, Morocco, Mozambique, Niger, Nigeria, Rwanda, the Seychelles, Sierra Leone, South Sudan, Tanzania, Togo and Tunisia. And they must do so, in order to *look like* a State in the eyes of the hegemonic world powers. Indeed, a number of the access to information laws and bills are limited in the extent to which they promote an actual culture of openness, suggesting that their passing may be somewhat superficial. The Kenyan access to information law (The Access to Information Act, 2016), for example, does not include an internal review mechanism for appealing access to information requests which are ignored or denied. In addition, the formulation of the public interest override clause is limited by discretionary language, which has the potential to significantly affect the disclosure of information which may in fact be in the public interest (2016: Section 6(4)). The Ghanaian access to information bill similarly contains limitations within its public interest override clause (Adu, 2013: 798).

Besides the OGP, the conditions of transparency imposed in foreign aid agreements can also suggest a global proselytisation of transparency by Western powers. Consider the conversation with the then UK Minister of State in the Department of International Development, Alan Duncan, regarding the role of the UK in promoting transparency in multilateral aid agreements in 2012:

> Q15: [...] To what extent can we impose, or de facto impose, those conditions of transparency, particularly at grass–roots level?
>
> Mr Duncan: You are absolutely right about the premium we set by transparency. In all the discussions, negotiations, or exercises of influence that we may have on any institution, we press the importance of transparency. Can we impose or dictate in all cases? Of course not. Can we wheedle it out of some institutions and make progress? Yes, and wherever we can, we do.
>
> On the EU for instance, it is complicated by treaty obligations and the as yet uncomplicated architecture of the External Action Service. Within the EU, we want to fight strongly to keep the European Development Fund separate, so that we can have greater influence over the element of funding that is specifically directed to impoverished countries.
>
> We in the DfID [Department for International Development] are setting a good example on transparency in everything we do internally and setting up the ODA [Official Development Assistance] Watchdog, and everything else. We are certainly not pretending when we say that we want transparency in other institutions; we are demanding it wherever we can.
>
> [...] We say, "we'll give you some core funding in principle, but we'll hold it back until you improve yourselves", be it against a transparency measure or a cost or efficiency measure.

This conversation makes explicit the objectives of the UK government to, in their own words, 'impose [...] conditions of transparency' (my emphasis) upon countries receiving aid. In doing so, the UK government claims transparency as 'its' value: it claims itself to be the hegemonic author of this discourse. Note also the Gramscian means by which the UK government seeks to 'impose' transparency: not through explicit violence, but through the tacit agreement which Gramsci (1999) lays out as the central means by which hegemony is appropriated: '[c]an we impose or dictate in all cases? Of course not. Can we wheedle it out of some institutions and make progress? Yes, and wherever we can, we do'. While this is suggestive of the way in which transparency is proselytised by the West through the rest of the world, it is also revealing of the way in which the discourse of transparency normalises, requiring less transparent states to 'improve [them]selves', to meet the unquestioned and inevitable ideal of transparency. Achille Mbembe – one of the leading thinkers on the postcolony (the world space after formal decolonisation has taken place) – critiques the imposition of Western discourse on the African region. Pertinent to the discussion here, he writes:

> Mired in the demands of what is immediately useful, enclosed in the narrow horizon of 'good governance' and the neo–liberal catechism about the market economy, torn by the current fads for 'civil society,' 'conflict resolution,' and alleged 'transitions to democracy', the discussion, as habitually engaged, is primarily concerned, not with comprehending the political in Africa or with producing knowledge in general, but with social engineering.
>
> (2001: 7)

For Mbembe, transparency would feature amongst the dominant discourses of development, democracy, economic growth and modernisation, which are reductionist and postulate as entirely independent from local realities, context and history. Critically these discourses work to – as he states – 'undermine the very possibility of understanding African economics and political facts' (2001: 7) in a move that is utterly reminiscent of the epistemic violence which rewrote the history and future path of colonial administrations in the 20th century.

Summary

Transparency is a powerful sign, loaded with particular powerful values which hold the ability to create and to shape other phenomena to which they are associated. As a discourse, transparency rests on a number of pre-conceived (and Western) categories of reason in order to outwardly project itself as universal (inclusive) and natural (a priori). One of the most powerful of these is the idea of democracy. As such, the discourse of transparency has sought, through the re-iteration of its statements, to fix the meaning of democracy, such that a State which does not make a claim to transparency is considered both undemocratic and illegitimate. But, simultaneously, this gives the transparency discourse its raison d'être, (in the words of Alan Duncan of the UK Government) 'to improve' and to be proselytised upon States which have not, as yet, declared their commitment to the ideals of transparency (and particularly the African region) through a process of what I have spoken of here as epistemic violence.

Notes

1 I use the word 'marginalises' cautiously, noting Spivak's comment that the so called 'marginalised' are, rather, the 'silent, silenced centre' (1993: 78).
2 I use the word "hegemonic" in the sense set out by Antonio Gramsci (1999), noting the differences between Gramsci and Foucault's conception of power. For Gramsci power is ideological, performed at a macro-level upon the ruled by the rulers, whereas Foucault imagined power as a relational yet ubiquitous phenomenon: enacted through discourse, power shapes reality and governs subjectivities. In particular, I draw on the idea that the ideas of the bourgeoisie (or dominant class or power structure) controls and totalises the production of discourse; and also the idea that hegemony takes place not through war or violent domination, but through tacit agreement. See also Bates (1975) and Daldal (2014).

Further reading

Adu, K. K. 2013. Ghana's Right to Information Bill: An Opportunity for the Implementation of Digital Preservation Infrastructure. *Journal of Emerging Trends in Computing and Information Sciences* 34(4): 748–763.

Barthes, R. 1972. *Mythologies*. Trans. A. Lavers. New York: Farrar, Straus & Giroux.

Bates, T. R. 1975. Gramsci and the Theory of Hegemony. *Journal of the History of Ideas* 36(2): 351–366.

Bianchi, A., & and Peters, A. 2013. *Transparency in International Law*. Cambridge: Cambridge University Press.

Birchall, C. 2011. The Politics of Opacity and Openness: Introduction to 'Transparency. *Theory, Culture and Society* 28(7–8): 7–25.

Clinton, H. 2012. US Senate Hearing on the 2012 Benghazi Consulate Attack. Available from: www.c-span.org/video/?c4529874/secretary-state-hillary-clinton-believe-transparency. [Accessed 13 August 2019].

Daldal, A. 2014. Power and Ideology in Michel Foucault and Antonio Gramsci: A Comparative Analysis. *Review of History and Political Science* 2(2): 149–167.

Erkkila, T. 2010. Transparenz, Transparency and Nordic Openness. In S. A. Jansen, E. Schröter & N. Stehr. (eds). *Transparenz: Multidisziplinäre Durchsichten durch Phänomene und Theorien des Undurchsichtigen*. Wiesbaden, Germany: VS Verlag, pp. 348–372.

Foucault, M. 1972. *Archaeology of Knowledge and the Discourse on Language*. Trans. A. M. Sheridan Smith. New York: Pantheon Books.

Foucault, M. 1980. Intellectuals and Power: A Conversation between Michel Foucault and Gilles Deleuze. In D. F. Bouchard (ed). *Language, Counter-Memory, Practice: Selected Essays and Interviews by Michel Foucault.* New York: Cornell University Press, pp. 205–217.

Glenn, H. P. 2014. Transparency and Closure. In R. G. Vaugn & P. Ala'i (eds). *Research Handbook on Transparency.* Cheltenham: Edward Elgar Publishing, pp. 15–29.

Gramsci, A. 1999. *Selections from the Prison Notebooks.* Trans. Q. Hoare & G. Nowell. London: Elec Books.

Lacan, J. 2007. *The Seminar of Jacques Lacan Book XVII: The Other Side of Psychoanalysis.* Trans. R. Grigg. New York: W. W. Norton.

Lessig, L. 2009. Against Transparency. *The New Republic* 1. Available from: https://newrepublic.com/article/70097/against-transparency

Mbembe, A. 2001. *On the Post-Colony.* Berkeley: University of California Press.

Ngwenya, M. 2018. Compliance through Decoration: Access to Information in Zimbabwe. In O. Shyllon (ed). *The Model Law on Access to Information for Africa and Other Regional Instruments: Soft Law and Human Rights in Africa.* Pretoria: Pretoria University Law Press, pp. 143–164.

Open Government Partnership. 2011. Open Government Declaration. Available from: www.opengovpartnership.org/open-government-declaration. [Accessed 15 August 2019].

Republic of Kenya. 2016. Access to Information Act, 31 of 2016. Available from: www.cuk.ac.ke/wp-content/uploads/2018/04/Access-to-Information-ActNo31.pdf. [Accessed 16 August 2019].

Roberts, J. 2009. No One is Perfect: The Limits of Transparency and an Ethic for 'Intelligent' Accountability. *Accounting, Organizations and Society* 34(8): 957–970.

Spivak, G. C. 1993. Can the Subaltern Speak? In L. Chrisman & P. Williams (eds). *Colonial Discourse and Post-Colonial Theory: A Reader.* Hemel Hempstead: Harvester, pp. 66–111.

Turilli. M, & Floridi, L. 2009. The Ethics of Information Transparency. *Ethics Information Technology* 11(2): 105–112.

United Kingdom, House of Commons, International Development Committee. 2010. *The World Bank: 4th Report of Session 2010–11, Volume 1,* HC 606. Minutes of 23 November 2010 of International Development Committee, Evidence 5.

United Nations Commission on International Trade Law. 2014. Rules of Transparency in Treaty-Based Investor-State Arbitration (effective 1 April 2014). Available from: www.uncitral.org/pdf/english/texts/arbitration/rules-on-transparency/Rules-on-Transparency-E.pdf. [Accessed 18 August 2019].

United Nations Economic Commission for Europe, Convention on Access to Information, Public Participation in Decision-Making and Access to Justice in Environmental Matters. 1998. Available from: www.unece.org/fileadmin/DAM/env/pp/documents/cep43e.pdf. [Accessed 6 December 2019].

Ward, G. 2014. *Unbelievable: Why We Believe and Why We Don't.* London: I. B. Taurus.

Part II
Towards the post-transparent

4 The fallacies of transparency

Fake news, artificial
intelligence and the
hyperinformation society

Introduction

> [It] results not from the lack of information but from information
> itself and even from an excess of information.
>
> (Baudrillard, 1985: 580)

If transparency stood for the call for the greater liberalisation of
information – premised on a value-laden model of openness to be
achieved through the public release of information, data and text – then
the idea of transparency must be understood as a central component
of our contemporary information society and the informational crises
it has generated. Yet, transparency offers a promise far greater than
simply liberalised information, and a lot of it; it offers a society that can
be seen, known, understood, and even changed, by those who are not
central to its construction, by the not-so-powerful. Transparency offers
the promise of a simpler world in which all can participate, equally,
through the shared possession of readily available information and
knowledge. The digital milieu and its offering of automated transparency, facilitates an even greater realisation of transparency's aims, with
the internet allowing, as Helen Margetts has commented, 'citizens to
take transparency into their own hands' (2011: 520). Information on
almost anything has become available immediately. In fact, with the
internet, not only was information made radically available to all,
anywhere, but information was rapidly produced: in the last two years
more information has been produced than between the dawn of man
and 2016, with this trajectory only increasing (Marr, 2018). The digitalisation of transparency through the internet and related technologies
brought about access to and the availability of all sorts of information
but, too, generated information on a mass scale, meaning that there
was – quite suddenly – far more to be known and therefore accessed.

In this information society, where the production, appropriation and exchange of information constitutes and perpetuates global society – transparency has become radicalised, on its own terms. But instead of resulting in the promised open society – a kind of secularised eschaton where all could be seen, known and understood – this new level of transparency, and the technologies it relies upon, has brought about new forms of closure, secrecy and opacity. Some of the ills of this new milieu have been readily recognised: loss of privacy, rampant and discriminatory surveillance, the attention economy, and fake news or disinformation, to name just a few. Yet, the response to these concerns in law and policy has been to call for further transparency. With respect to artificial intelligence (AI)-driven technologies, transparency constitutes a key ethical response from policy-makers and firms, in an almost ironic overlooking of the fact that much of AI's processing powers and algorithmic decision-making is simply impenetrable to human minds given the mass scale on which it takes place.

This chapter explores this last phenomenon, fake news, within the context of the diachronic historical arc of the discourse of transparency. For Foucault, it is in these moments of discontinuity and transformation, when the objectives and meanings of a discourse appear to shift (like the shift from the literal to the metaphoric use of transparency traced in Chapter 1), that we can analyse the workings of power. This is the very task of the genealogist – not 'to trace the gradual curve of their [the discursive statement] evolution, but to isolate the different scenes where they engaged in different roles' (Foucault, 1971: 77). Thus, we trace the evolution of transparency from its global status as a value of a Western notion of liberal and open governance, to what I describe here as its illusory form. I draw on the post-modernist writings of Jean Baudrillard to extend my critique and explore the contours of what he calls a hyperinformation society. The discussions here expose two fallacies of transparency. The first, brought to light by the phenomenon of fake news, is transparency's assumption that the information it would put into circulation would be true, or at the very least, real. The second fallacy relates more broadly to the discursive construct of transparency itself: that transparency is merely an illusion to comfort citizens and allow us to believe we have access to the forces of power that act upon us.

Fake news: Baudrillard and the hyperinformation society

Today, "fake news" has become a ubiquitous term. Itself a misnomer, the term is broadly understood within policy discourse to be both inadequate and misleading, as recognised by in the European Union's (EU) recent report on online disinformation. Without any specific reference to Trumpism, the EU report goes on to name fake news as 'a weapon with which powerful actors can interfere in circulation of information and attack and undermine independent news media', (2018: 10) ultimately causing a breach of 'constitutional integrity' and 'a risk for democracy' (2018: 12). As an alternative, the EU High Level Expert Group, who authored and compiled the report, use the term 'disinformation', which they broadly define as 'all forms of false, inaccurate, or misleading information designed, presented and promoted to intentionally cause public harm or for profit' (2018: 11). The EU report sets out five key principles, or pillars, upon which a response to disinformation should be established. With the word mentioned on almost every page of the report, the first pillar is 'increased transparency' (2018). The report calls for transparency to enhance the intelligibility of different types of digital information sources (2018: 6), transparency for online advertising and sponsored content (2018: 15–16), transparency for fact checking (2018: 16), transparency for algorithmic processing (2018: 16), and transparency for media ownership (2018: 19), to name just a few. In addition, in discussing best practices for tacking online disinformation, transparency is listed as the first category of 'good practices'; in comparison, 'bad practices' include a 'lack of transparency' (2018: 14). Like in other policy documents discussed in previous chapters, the notion of transparency in the EU report is taken as a given and rendered beyond critique. Instead, transparency is conceived in terms of the following:

> Transparency is a key element in the response to digital disinformation. It is a cross-cutting issue that concerns the whole digital media value chain and aims at making news production and distribution less opaque with a view to supporting users' ability to better discern between journalistic quality content and various kinds of disinformation.
>
> (EU, 2018: 22)

Yet, as the report itself notes, the phenomenon of "fake news" is interrelated to the new ways in which information is produced, distributed and engaged with in the digital economy, including through digital media and platforms, such as Google and Facebook. Putting this rather more critically, and "fake news" can be understood as a kind of cancerous growth of the information society of which transparency is a key proponent. These linkages between notions of transparency and the liberalisation of information, and the production and circulation of information which ultimately undermines the very objectives of the transparency project, have received little critical attention.

Over 30 years ago, Jean Baudrillard was already contemplating the deficiencies of a growing information society. Writing at a time when personal computers were increasingly becoming a household necessity, when John de Mol was conceiving of Big Brother for UK Channel 4, and in what David Kamp describes as the tabloid decade with 'the tabloidification of news, culture and even human behaviour' (1999), Baudrillard's insights are remarkably farsighted. One of his key contributions is his idea of 'hyperreality', which he first developed in *Simulacra and Simulation* (1981). Baudrillard arrives at the idea of a hyperreality having set out the concepts of simulacra and simulation. In short, simulacra can be understood as the sign of a lost reality or a reality that was never there to begin with, where simulation is the state of the hyperreal where reality consists of a constant replay and reconstitution of the signs of reality, such that the sign becomes reality itself (1981). As such, hyperreality names a historical condition wherein the real has been overtaken by reproductions and representations of reality: the real becomes indistinguishable from its representation; what is true becomes indistinguishable from what is false or fake; and meaning is irreparably lost in the endless orbit of communication and disclosure, sharing and click-bait.

More pertinently, Baudrillard associates the descent into hyperreality with the media and informationism. In a uncannily titled essay, 'The Masses: The implosion of the Social in the Media', published in 1985, Baudrillard writes: 'we will never in future be able to separate reality from its statistical, simulative projection in the media, a state of suspense and of definitive uncertainty about reality' (579). He goes on to analyse the uncertainty which characterises the hyperreal as a product of the informationism generated by mass media: '[it] results not from the lack of information but from information itself and even from an excess of information' (1985: 580). The result is the futility of simulation:

> Overinformed, it [the masses] develops ingrowing obesity. For everything which loses its *scene* (like the obese body) becomes for that very reason ob-*scene.*
>
> The silence of the masses is also in a sense obscene. For the masses are also made of this useless hyperinformation which claims to enlighten them, when all it does is clutter up the space of the representable and annul itself in a silent equivalence. And we

cannot do much against this obscene circularity of the masses and of information. The two phenomena fit one another: the masses have no opinion and information does not inform them.

(Italics in original, 1985: 580)

With 'information [that] does not inform', and the pointless proliferation of information in the mass media and elsewhere, the symbolic exchange of face to face communication is disrupted, instead producing the constant simulation of meaning. In this simulation or hyperreality, meaning and reality has, as suggested by Mark Poster in his Introduction to Baudrillard's work, 'no referent, no ground, no source. It operates outside the logic of representation' (1988: 7).

Significant, too, is Baudrillard's emphasis of the obscene. From the Latin *ob* denoting 'to stand in the way of', and *'scene'* as the place of meaning-making (also *obscène* in the original French), meaning is entirely dispersed in the violence of the hyperreal. In the description above, this obscenity becomes a feature of 'the masses' themselves, and what is produced is the impassive and depoliticising uncertainty where 'the masses have no opinion and information does not inform them' (Baudrillard, 1985: 580), as information is itself a simulation of truth and meaning, an illusion of itself. Moreover, this state of obscenity is historically marked by what Baudrillard refers to as 'transparence and immediate visibility':

> Obscenity begins precisely when there is no more spectacle, no more scene, when all becomes transparence and immediate visibility, when everything is exposed to the harsh and inexorable light of information and communication. [...] It is no longer then the traditional obscenity of what is hidden, repressed, forbidden or obscure; on the contrary, it is the obscenity of the visible, of the all-too-visible, of the more-visible-than-the-visible. It is the obscenity of what no longer has any secret, of what dissolves completely in information and communication.
>
> (1983: 130–131)

In the hyperbolic state of transparency, the secret – and with it meaning in general – has been annihilated by too much information and communication, by too much visibility, too much transparency.

By the publication of Baudrillard's later book *The Transparency of Evil* in 1990, the endless reproduction of signs and simulation marks an interminable depoliticisation, expressly because the political has already happened: we are now 'after the orgy' (3). But, as Baudrillard readily articulates, 'what do we do now the orgy is over?' (1990: 3) His response is further simulation:

> We may pretend to carry on in the same direction, accelerating, but in reality we are accelerating into a void, because all the goals of liberation are already behind us, and because what haunts and obsesses us is being thus ahead of all the results — the very availability of all the signs, all the forms, all the desires that we had been pursuing. But what can we do? This is the state of simulation, a state in which we are obliged to replay all scenarios precisely because they have all taken place already, whether actually or potentially. The state of utopia realized, wherein paradoxically we must continue to live as though they had not been. But since they have, and since we can no longer, therefore, nourish the hope of realizing them, we can only 'hyper-realize' them through interminable simulation.

At this point we reach an impasse. Baudrillard offers no further elucidations: the exchange of signs continues ad infinitum, and with it disappears, or disperses, other contingencies and possibilities within which any kind of resistance or repoliticisation can be kindled. Somewhat differently, Clare Birchall's critique of the information society is not that its effects are depoliticising, but rather *anti*politicising (2017). For Birchall, this term more adequately captures the way in which the information society intimates a radical realisation of democracy's objectives of individual empowerment and political participation, yet concurrently forecloses these opportunities and freedoms through positioning the citizen as a consumer (2017). Within this framing, the possibility of resistance and repoliticisation remains. But Baudrillard simply exhausts – a point taken up in the interviews with Sylvère Lotringer published in Baudrillard's *Forget Foucault* (1998). Critique is exhausted not because it is taken to its limits as such, but because critique becomes consumed – overtaken – by a new schematic of exchange and simulation which, according to its logic, is ahistorical, apolitical and without alternative.

To follow Baudrillard's thinking precisely and to accede that critique no longer serves any purpose, would render the exercise undertaken here futile. Yet, Baudrillard's prophetic analysis of a hyperinformed society where information no longer informs and where truth is indistinguishable from its counterfeit simulacra, becomes recognisable within today's climate of fake news and disinformation. Within this milieu, transparency is radicalised to the point where it begins to undo itself, and the information it liberalises can no longer be assumed to be true, or at the very least, real. Thus, with fake news and disinformation, the discursive fallacies upon which transparency was based are exposed. It is this moment that I refer to as the post-transparent, where transparency functions as an empty simulation, and can no longer fulfil on its promise in part because that promise has already been fulfilled, and in part because it is part of the discursive architecture of the digitalised information society which has generated new levels of opacity and illegibility. The next section turns to explore the political function of transparency as a simulation or illusion, arguing that it works as a kind of Nietzschean (Nietzsche, 2006) self-comforting narrative that, as a response to the growing complexity and opacity of today's society, allows citizens to believe that the society in which they live is understandable, accessible and, ultimately, intractable.

The illusion of transparency

Disinformation is but one aspect of an increasingly complex digital eco-system. Central to this system is artificial intelligence (AI), which can operate only with the real-time availability of massive amounts of data. Made possible by (and continuously compounding) a 'transparent society' where data and information about (almost) anything is collected instantaneously, many of these AI-driven data systems are simply impenetrable. This is because they both operate on such a large scale and involve complex layers of data sharing and algorithmic processing, and because the deep learning technologies involved in these systems are inherently opaque. It is for this reason that within computing, the deeply coded and layered place in which the data inputs are converted into data outputs takes place, is called the black box – because how the algorithm's decisions are arrived at are simply incomprehensible for the human mind to pinpoint and decipher (Pasquale, 2015).

Both Pasquale and Zuboff have explored the growing complexity of our digital society, the understanding of which is increasingly concentrated in the hands of a few. From finance and the behaviour of the stock markets, to the delivery of health care, the monitoring of employees and the use of search engines, Pasquale describes a highly convoluted digital system whose triggers can be readily manipulated by those in power to exploit those who have a limited understanding of the data-driven powers which are increasingly governing their lives. purposely crafted to render citizens qua consumers in the dark. This 'one-way mirror', as he calls it, is characterised by powerful bodies (mostly corporate, but state too) that have 'unprecedented knowledge of the minutiae of our daily lives, while we know little to nothing about how they use this knowledge to influence the important decision that we – and they – make' (2015: 9). He considers how, in such conditions, the Internet's original promise of transparency and a re-balancing of information/power asymmetries has instead manifested in exponential obfuscation and exploitation (2015: 13–14).

For Zuboff, in her quickly classic text *The Age of Surveillance Capitalism* (2018), the multi-layered systems of digital accumulation that collect, take and scrape personal data of one kind or another, constitutes a threat to humanity itself, as such technologies work to control and nudge human (read: consumer) behaviour and experience. This new world order she calls surveillance capitalism, premised on new arrangements of knowledge accumulation and freedom. She writes that within surveillance capitalism, 'the combination of knowledge and freedom works to accelerate the asymmetry of power between surveillance capitalists and the societies in which they operate' (2018: 499). The more knowledge held by the surveillance capitalists, the less individuals and societies know. The system is predicated on the ignorance of those from whom knowledge (personal information and data) is collected. Zuboff names one of the key ways in which this system works as 'the problem of two texts' (2018: 186). The first text is the public-facing text we consume and contribute to as we engage with the surface images, blog posts, tweets, clicks and all other material readily given to us, and which we readily give, online. This text is the text which purports to create participatory democracy, where all can enjoy the benefits of freely available knowledge and information. This text is where the material disclosures of public transparency lie: where institutions claim to be transparent by providing access to information about their activities, people and profits. But this text is not all that is taking place. Behind the first text is a second, shadow, text, which only the surveillance capitalists have access to. The first text operates as the supply operation for the shadow text: 'everything that we contribute to the first text, no matter how trivial or fleeting, becomes a target for surplus extraction' (2019: 186). Thus, this second text, Zuboff describes, 'is a burgeoning accumulation of behavioural surplus and its analyses, and it says more about us than we can know about ourselves' (2018: 186). The knowledge that surveillance capitalists – like Google and Facebook – derive from the second text gets fed back into the first text in order to control and nudge the behaviour that is recorded in the first text. 'When it comes to the shadow text', Zuboff writes, 'surveillance capitalism's laws of motion compel both its secrecy and its continuous growth. We are the objects of its narratives, from whose lessons we are excluded' (2018: 187).

Within both Zuboff and Pasquale's rendering of our information society and its forms of obfuscation, law plays an essential role in allowing the status quo to continue ad infinitum. With respect of transparency laws, Pasquale describes how such laws have been used for deliberately antithetical purposes to what they were supposedly designed, with public or private bodies, for example, responding to an access to information request by providing millions of documents which the requester must then sift through and interpret (2015: 7). For Zuboff, privacy laws and standards, in particular, have been ineffective in protecting individuals' online privacy. In fact, she notes how "compliance" with such laws have been used in such a way that individuals are structurally excluded from ever having any meaningful knowledge – let alone control – as to how their data is collected and used, through the oppressive and binary use of "terms-of-service agreements", wherein individuals are forced to hand over access to their personal data or have no access to the product, service, or website they are seeking to use (2018: 48–50). Indeed, as one study from 2008 found that it would take 76 full workdays to read all of the privacy terms and policies individuals come across in a given year (Zuboff, 2018: 50). Zuboff notes that 'the numbers are much higher today' (2018: 50).

In an increasingly complex and secretive information driven society, transparency remains a central value both claimed and called for. The policy responses to issues such as "fake news", privacy and data protection, or the opacity of AI-driven data technologies and even the social harms – including bias and discrimination – produced by AI-related technologies, has been a demand for even greater transparency. A study published with *Nature Machine Intelligence* which mapped the global landscape of ethics policies and guidelines found that "transparency" was the most popular 'ethical value' listed in such documents, appearing in 73 out of 84 policies reviewed (Jobin, Lenca & Vayena, 2019). Why is this? What role do these claims and calls for transparency play in a progressively more opaque society? And, if as was explored in the previous section, transparency's claims are becoming redundant, what function does its discourse serve? What I suggest is that the function of the discourse of transparency is to allow citizens to feel empowered in our ever more complex societies, to have reason to believe that the forces that act upon us can be seen, known, accessed and understood.

In his book of 1998, *Seeing like a State: How Certain Schemes to Improve the Human Condition Have Failed*, James Scott argued that the modern bureaucratic state seeks to make society legible through the over-simplification of its complexities. Based on his critique of high modernity – which would alternatively be referred to today as technological determinism: the normative idea that science and technology provide the ultimate and objective basis from which all governance and decision-making should take place – this simplification is what allows states to enact political control over its subjects (1998). It is, too, the model of statehood that was perfected by European states through colonialism: such imperial society planning, Scott argues, 'excludes the necessary role of local knowledge and know-how' (1998: 6), in a move similar to how I have described, in the previous chapters, the foreclosure of other forms of knowledge and governance through the globalisation of the discourse of transparency. For Scott, the state seeks to make society simpler in order to make it legible, manageable and, ultimately, controllable. With transparency, however, the objective is to make the state itself appear more legible. The illusion of transparency is that it allows citizens to believe that the forces of power that act upon them are (or can be made) accessible, legible, visible and trustworthy. This belief is achieved through the illusion of a transparent society – of an immediacy in the relationship between state and its citizens, and a state that is visible to its citizens – produced through the presence of transparency laws and standards, and through the calls to and claims for transparency globally enunciated.

More precisely, the idea of "the illusion of transparency" is a heuristic that names the way in which the discursive construct of transparency works in an imaginary – or illusive – way to create the idea of a world that can be seen, known, accessed and, ultimately, changed. In arguing that transparency is an illusion, I am not saying that transparency is itself futile, empty and meaningless, and therefore without political effects. Its political effects are real and material, as has been explored in previous chapters and as will be explored with respect to individuals and subjectivity in the following chapter. It is rather that transparency's claims are shown to be empty – operating within the logic of their own discourse. For Friedrich Nietzsche, this has always been the condition of human societies. We create narratives which comfort us and our place in the world, and claim these narratives are transcendental a priori truths that we have not ourselves created, but which are arrived at through knowledge, science, or even religion. In his famous treatise, 'On Truth and Lies in the Nonmoral Sense', Nietzsche writes that we 'are deeply immersed in illusions and in dream images; [our] eyes merely glide over the surface of things and see 'forms'' (2006: 115).

Access to information laws expose the illusion of transparency rather more mechanically. Typically, access to information laws exist as part of a states' regulatory transparency infrastructure. However, as has been noted with respect to access to information laws (and discussed in Chapter 2), the disclosure of information is a long and bureaucratic process (Darch & Underwood, 2005) and, too, requires citizens to deferentially "request" "access" to state records. In practice, access to information laws are often not adequately complied with, and are limited in reach as they do not extend to the private sector (Darch & Underwood, 2010). Yet, despite this, they are essential for governments to appear transparent and to gain the legitimacy that this claim to transparency affords. (An example here is the OGP, discussed in detail in the previous chapter, wherein countries can only join and participate if they have an access to information law). Thus, an access to information law is essential for a government to create the appearance of transparency, both in terms of their legitimacy within the international community, but also – and perhaps more critically – in order to promote citizen's belief that they can access state information and that transparency, or the control of information flows, ultimately lies in the hands of the citizenry. Instead, the disclosure of state and private sector information happens far less often from access to information requests at the hands of citizens, and far more often in the form of voluntary (and often automatic or electronic) disclosures by the state or private sector itself, where such bodies can control the content, form, and timing of what is released, and where the labour performed in, and political intentions of, such transactions can be abstracted and concealed in a cloud of technological neutrality. In this sense, transparency then becomes a political strategy for underplaying institutional power and allowing for the idea that the institution in question can be changed, accessed, understood, and made accountable to, those which it holds power over: a model which seems only to be intensifying with the growing complexity of our digital society.

Summary

In this chapter, we have explored the growing complexities of our information society and the continued call for and claim to transparency that resounds within it. I have drawn on the phenomenon of fake news as an illustration of transparency's fallacies becoming unravelled. For Baudrillard, as discussed, there will come a time when the distinction between reality and its simulation – between real and fake – elides and the differences between them becomes indistinguishable. In some sense we can see Baudrillard's prophesy taking shape with fake news and indeed even deep fakes – wherein AI techniques are applied to overlay images and films with non-original content (Beridze & Butcher, 2019). More broadly, however, the growing complexities of our information society, and the intensifying calls for and claims to transparency in law and policy, reveal a tension in the discursive construct and function of transparency. What I have argued here is that transparency functions within this current milieu to comfort citizens with the idea that we can see, know, and understand the powers that act on us, through the use of transparency mechanisms. Yet, these mechanisms are, to an extent, empty and meaningless, rendering transparency as an illusion or fallacy. Moreover, with limited knowledge of the ways in which the system operates and force a transparency from its citizens through data collection and surveillance (more on this in the next chapter), such systems can more effectively nudge and control our behaviour, behind the veil that transparency laws and standards offer.

Further reading

Adams, R. 2017. Key Concepts: Michel Foucault Biopolitics/Biopower. Available from: http://criticallegalthinking.com/2017/05/10/michel-foucault-biopolitics-biopower/ [Accessed 5 September 2019].

Baudrillard, J. 1981. *Simulacra and Simulation*. Michigan: University of Michigan Press.

Baudrillard, J. 1983. The Ecstasy of Communication. In H Foster (ed). *The Anti-Aesthetic: Essays on Postmodern Culture*. Washington: Bay Press, pp. 126–134.

Baudrillard, J. 1985. The Masses: The Implosion of the Social in the Media. *New Literary History* 16(3): 577–589.

Baudrillard, J. 1990. *The Transparency of Evil: Essays on Extreme Phenomena*. London: Verso.

Baudrillard, J. 1998. *Forget Foucault*. Cambridge: MIT Press.

Beridze, I., & Butcher, J. 2019. When Seeing if No Longer Believing. *Nature Machine Intelligence* 1: 332–334.

Darch, C., & Underwood, P. G. 2005. Freedom of Information Legislation, State Compliance and the Discourse of Knowledge: The South African Experience. *The International Information & Library Review* 37(2): 77–86.

Darch, C., & Underwood, P. G. 2010. *Freedom of Information and the Developing World: The Citizen, the State and Models of Openness*. Oxford: Chandos Publishing.

European Union. 2018. Report on Fake News and Online Disinformation. Available from: www.tgcom24.mediaset.it/binary/documento/97.$plit/C_2_documento_1140_upfDocumento.pdf. [Accessed 26 August 2019].

Foucault, M. 1971. Nietzsche, Genealogy, History. In P. Rabinow (ed). *The Foucault Reader*. New York: Pantheon Books, pp. 76–100.

Foucault, M. 1998. *The Will to Knowledge: History of Sexuality Volume I.* Trans. R. Hurley. London: Penguin.

Golder, B., & Fitzpatrick, P. 2009. *Foucault's Law*. London: Routledge.

Jobin, A., Ienca, M., & Vayena, E. 2019. The Global Landscape of AI Ethics Guidelines. *Nature Machine Intelligence* 1: 389–399.

Kamp, D. 1999. The Tabloid Decade. *Vanity Fair*. Available from: www.vanityfair.com/culture/1999/02/david-kamp-tabloid-decade [Accessed 26 August 2019].

Margetts, H. 2011. The Internet and Transparency. *The Political Quarterly* 84(4): 518–521.

Marr, B. 2018. How Much Data Do We Create Every Day? The Mind-Blowing Stats Everyone Should Read. *Forbes*. Available from: www.forbes.com/sites/bernardmarr/2018/05/21/how-much-data-do-we-create-every-day-the-mind-blowing-stats-everyone-should-read/#76c0603360ba. [Accessed 18 August 2019].

Nietzsche, F. 2006. On Truth and Lies in a Nonmoral Sense. In K. Ansell-Pearson & D. Large (eds). *The Nietzsche Reader*. London: Blackwell Publishing, pp. 114–120.

Pasquale, F. 2015. *The Blackbox Society: The Secret Algorithms that Control Money and Information*. Cambridge, MA: Harvard University Press.

Poster, M. 1988. Introduction. In M. Poster (ed). *Jean Baudrillard Selected Writings*. Stanford, CA: Stanford University Press, pp. 1–11.

Scott, J. 1998. *Seeing Like a State: How Certain Schemes to Improve the Human Condition Have Failed*. New Haven, CT and London: Yale University Press.

Zuboff, S. 2018. *The Age of Surveillance Capitalism: The Fight for a Human Future at the New Frontier of Power*. London: Profile Books.

5 Producing the transparent subject

The gaze turns inward

Introduction

> Why in this great system of relations of power has a régime of truth developed indexed to subjectivity? Why does power require [...] individuals to say not only, 'here I am, me who obeys,' but in addition, 'this is what I am, me who obeys, this is who I am, this is what I have seen, this is what I have done'?
>
> (Foucault, 2014: 82)

The recent history of our information age has been marked by singular events whereby individual whistle-blowers have revealed the extensive, intrusive and totalitarian ways in which governments and powerful organisations collect and analyse personal data. Such events include Edward Snowden's disclosure of US National Security Agency highly classified documents showing the extent of citizen surveillance in 2013 and the Cambridge Analytica scandal of 2018, which revealed the use of big data analytics, profiling and targeted/personalised advertising in the 2016 US Presidential campaign.[1]

Together these events signalled that the discourse of transparency materialises on the bodies of citizens and individuals. But at once, the revelations of Snowden and Cambridge Analytica also constituted a concealment, for these disclosures presupposed the wilful forgetting of our own self-offering in the reiteration of the transparency discourse, our own 'putting oneself into discourse' (Foucault, 2014: 307). Again, a comforting narrative is constructed: just as transparency allows us to believe we can see and know the forces of power that act upon us (as discussed in the previous chapter), the narratives of Snowden and Cambridge Analytica allowed us to forget that we participate in transparency's conceit through self-disclosure.

In this chapter, then, I discuss the subject of the discourse of transparency. I draw on Foucault's ideas about subjectivity and 'acts of truth' (2014) in order to critique the way in which the modern subject is called upon – or interpellated (Althusser, 2001)[2] – to subjectivise herself to and within this discourse. I argue that transparency hails a discursive subject which participates within this dominant discourse through disclosure, whether through ever more sophisticated surveillance technologies, or through self-disclosing mechanisms such as social media and self-tracking devices. I explore, too, the role of various legislative regimes that promote or enforce a transparent subject, including the UK Investigatory Powers Act and legislation to ban the veil. In addition, I discuss idea of whistleblowing within this framework, examining it as an act of a certain truth in the whistle-blower's public manifestation and legitimisation of transparency's régime of truth.

Lastly, this chapter turns to explore the effects of the normalisation of a transparent subject. I contend that the acts of truths hailed by this discourse are depoliticising, containing the individual within the order of discourse and seeking to produce unmediated, unobjectionable and homogenous bodies, and eradicate difference and all that is hidden. In so doing, I posit depoliticisation to refer to the process of foreclosing and delimiting other possibilities (of subjectivity) besides that of the dominant discursive order of transparency, that is neoliberalism, noting that neoliberalism is itself depoliticising insofar as it is presented as inevitable and without alternative.[3]

Foucault and subjectivity

Foucault's work on subjectivity culminated in his last decade, and particularly in his lecture series delivered at the Collège de France.[4] In his earlier work, Foucault had articulated the 'docile body' as 'a body [...] that may be subjected, used, transformed, and improved' (1995: 136); it was fashioned externally by coercive and disciplining power, the subjectivised site whereupon discourse fought for domination. Yet, in his later work Foucault discusses further, and makes more complex, the relationship between discourse and subject. Foucault begins to contemplate a subject fashioned *internally* in obedience to dominant and institutionalised discourses through the outward manifestation of its discursive truths (2014). Thus, the practices of power which make the subject docile have turned inward, in a gesture of discursive self-performance. Docility is not lost, but is instead inwardly fashioned as the subject 'obeys' discourse. It is for this reason that Foucault speaks of 'putting *oneself* into discourse' (2014: 307) – my emphasis on the reflexive pronoun.

In *On the Government of the Living* lecture series, Foucault describes in some detail how the individual puts himself into institutionalised discourse through acts of truth which outwardly manifest its internalisation (2014). Foucault begins a genealogy back to antiquity and early Christian practices where subjects were called upon to undertake acts of truth in the form of confession and penitence. Through truth acts, the subject self-constructed its position as both *object of* and *subject to* the order of discourse, at once affirming his faith in the discursive 'régime of truth', that is, as a 'technique and procedure [...] for obtaining [and producing] truth' (Foucault, 1977: 13). In addition, the performance of truth acts led to the salvation of the self, allowing the self to encounter its true being (2014). Foucault argues that these acts of truth demonstrate an important historical moment in the constitution of the modern subject, a subject which self-fashions in obedience to the ephemeral rules of discourse and the discursive régime of truth. He describes thus:

> We are obliged to speak of ourselves in order to tell the truth of ourselves. In this obligation to speak about oneself you can see the eminent place taken by discourse. Putting oneself in discourse is in actual fact one of the major driving forces in the organization of subjectivity and truth relationships in the Christian West.
>
> (2014: 311)

Foucault's rumination on the 'obligation' to put oneself into discourse is revealing of the perpetual power relations that occur in the formation of the subject. Indeed, he goes on to state that 'this institutionalisation of truth/subjectivity relationships through the obligation to tell the truth about oneself [...] cannot be conceived without the existence and functioning of a form of power' (2014: 312); and asks:

> Why and how does the exercise of power in our society, the exercise of power as government of men, demand not only acts of obedience and submission, but truth acts in which individuals who are subjects in the power relationship are also subjects as actors, spectator witnesses, or objects in manifestation of truth procedures?
>
> (2014: 82)

The subject imposes her knowledge of discourse on herself through an inward-looking and scrupulous gaze, which constitutes an act of truth in terms of the logic of the discourse, and, at once, also an act of obedience. This obedience is essential for the salvation of the self, and becomes an ethical responsibility towards both society and oneself, which further strengthens and legitimises the dominant discourse whose 'truths' are then manifest in the subject. As such, the gaze of Foucault's earlier work – specifically *The Birth of the Clinic* (1973), where he espouses on the gaze of medical professions on patients which constituted the patient as the subject of knowledge, and *Discipline and Punish* (1995), where the gaze of power become a disciplinary measure to control and normalise the behaviour of those deemed outside of discourse (such as the mentally ill, and the criminal) – is turned inward.

The transparent subject

As a dominant cultural value, transparency has exceeded the field of institutional governance and has become an ethical imperative for the conduct of the self in society. It is the extension of a concept onto domains of society beyond that within which it was originally legitimated which, in Judith Butler's reading of Foucault, makes it illegitimate, and thus makes the exercise of its critique an ethical one (2002: 212).

Our present-day ethos demands that individuals be transparent to themselves, to their fellow citizens, and to institutions of power (State and non-state). Elizabeth Fisher recognises this in her critique of transparency when she notes that transparency entails normative assumptions about the behaviour of individuals in society (2014: 60–61). Indeed, Patrick Lee Plaisance, too, writes that 'transparent interaction is what allows us as rational, autonomous beings to assess each other's behaviour. Our motivations, aspirations and intents are fully set forth for examination' (2007: 187). He continues, saying that 'when we use deception or stop short of full disclosure, we fail to treat others with the requisite dignity and respect. We fail as moral beings, in effect' (2007: 187). Similarly, John Roberts notes that 'transparency [...] plays with my fears of being exposed and humiliated whilst at the same time encouraging me to take pride in what is disclosed' (2009: 958).

In order to fulfil on the ethics of transparency, we must make public acts of self-disclosures – the acts of truth of the transparency discourse. Through the performance of self-disclosures the subject becomes an ethical citizen, or, as Butler describes it in her reading of Foucault, a 'recognizable' form of being: one that is recognised as an individual by her society (2002: 22–26). The subject is therefore self-constitutes within a discursively produced régime of truth; and transparency's régime of truth demands acts of transparency by its citizens. Butler explains that this régime of truth is

> presented [by Foucault] as the available norms through which self–recognition can take place, so that what I can 'be', quite literally, is

constrained in advance by a régime of truth that decides what will and will not be a recognizable form of being.

(2002: 22)

It is in this way – by foreclosing other possible realities – that transparency normalises specific citizen behaviour, and produces a particular social order and cultural ethos based around self-disclosure.

Self-disclosure

The loss of privacy – of the individual's autonomy over where, when and how they are revealed to others – is a growing characteristic of our late information society. It can be broadly understood as one of the key informational crises of our times. I have discussed this to some extent in the previous chapter, by engaging particularly with Shoshana Zuboff's work on surveillance capitalism (2018). Indeed, with ever-growing technological capabilities which intrude in one way or another into an individual's physical, mental and digital space (including facial, gait, emotion and heartbeat recognition technologies), individual transparency to the powers which collect and analyse our personal data and information is not just intensifying but becoming the normal basis for ethical conduct. That this is the case is manifestly expressed in the sentiment of "nothing to hide". Those individuals who do not conform to the required level of transparency are thus assumed to have something to hide, to be something which is unwanted by dominant societal norms.

A number of studies have considered the idea of a transparent self both demanded and produced by contemporary society (including Award & Krishnan, 2006; Zur, Williams, Levahot & Knapp, 2009). Byung-Chul Han offers one of the more sustained critiques of the concept of transparency in his 2012 publication *The Transparent Society*. In his radical exposition on transparency, he insists that transparency represents a hegemonic and totalitarian ideology which has radically transformed social relations, and which is working towards the computerisation of humanity (2015). In fact, in this regard, Han's critique foreshadows the later work of Brett Frischmann and Evan Selinger in their well-acclaimed 2018 book *Re-Engineering Humanity*, which describes how AI and digital surveillant technologies are not only nudging our behaviour, but computerising it, turning us into predictable machines. For Han, however, the radical exposure which transparency demands, can be equated with pornography, where exposure is encouraged and commodified as part of the totalising forces of capitalism (2015).

Marjolein Lanzing, on the other hand, provides an alternate description of the modern self who, she argues, is made transparent through self-tracking technologies (2016). Lanzing points out that such technologies not only create individuals made transparent to themselves by recording and tracking personal information, but also encourages individuals to disclose and share this information to unspecified receivers. For Lanzing, the technologies used in such applications decontextualise personal information, such that 'information that was formerly confined to and aimed at a particular social context or relationship [...] transgress[es] its usual borders' (2016: 13). Lanzing ultimately argues that this constitutes a violation of privacy rights (2016). Like Lanzing, Marc Chrysanthou engages in a critique of the personal information rendered through health information products, services and applications and medical screenings (2002). For Chrysanthou – who explores the idea of the postmodern 'informed body' – these practices of self-tracking and surveillance as revealing what he terms 'a crisis of the embodied self in the age of information' (2002: 470). He explains how 'the Enlightenment dream of social progress through knowledge becomes, in the postmodern, a fantasy of bodily perfection through information' (2002: 470). For both Lanzing and Chrysanthou, the information society within which these subjectivities are created and encouraged provides an opportunity for intervention and control, all under the auspices of self-improvement, well-being, or to use Foucault's word, 'salvation' (2014).

Relatedly, Scott McQuire equates the rise of self-disclosure with a media-based 'performative' self, who exhibits in order to be publically evaluated, and, perhaps, accepted (or as Butler would say, 'recognized' (2002)) (2003: 119). He describes how, in this culture of disclosure, the technologies of control have been both internalised and then re-performed on television screens as entertainment, under the guise that 'giving up private space in the name of public entertainment [...offers...] a glimpse of a more open society with greater transparency in interpersonal relations' (2002: 119). However, as Scott notes, these 'softer' panoptic mechanisms 'of pleasurable viewing and consumption' work alongside 'harder' disciplinary forces of computerised surveillance and social policing' (2002: 119). Notably for the discussion here, Scott speaks of how the individual self-fashions within this transparent milieu, with constant feedback and appraisal, such that there arises 'a gradual embedding in consciousness of the concept of public "testing" of the performance of the private self' (2002: 119).

Like the self-tracking technologies discussed by Lanzing and Chrysanthou that create discursive opportunities for control and intervention, McQuire establishes that the mediatised performative self is subject to disciplinary mechanisms of control which have been normalised by a prevailing culture of transparency. Within this culture, the self is required to improve and 'perfect' itself through public disclosure and feedback, which, within the social media clime of today would equate to likes, re-shares and followers. For McQuire, however, this signals the loss of subjectivity formed in 'private' spaces and he asks whether this is a loss we should be mourning (2002: 110).

The call for the self to publicly testify and self-appraise can also be understood alongside Foucault's discussion of confession. Foucault's ideas are based around the French word for confession – *aveu* – which translates more broadly into English as avowal, admission and acknowledgement (2014: xvii). Confession stands as a public avowal, or act of truth, which reiterates the discursive régime of truth, revealing its internalisation within the subject (Elden, 2005). Through confession, subjects submit themselves to governance by the truth (2014). In *The Will to Knowledge: The History of Sexuality Volume I* Foucault extends the critique of confession to a critique of Western society writ large, remarking that 'the confession [has become] one of the West's most highly valued techniques for producing truth', and that 'when it is not spontaneous or dictated by some internal imperative, the confession is wrung from a person by violence or threat; it is driven from its hiding place in the soul, or extracted from the body' (1998: 59).

In today's transparent modernity, the operations of what Foucault calls our 'singularly confessing society' have intensified, as surveillance technologies are coupled with big data analytics, social media and, as discussed below, legislative regimes to ensure the citizen remains open to the gaze of the state. As the modern subject self-discloses (and we must note that this self-disclosure is not always wilful), it both manifests the discourse of transparency in its own revelations of truth, in its own disclosures of information and data, and reasserts transparency's legitimacy as the prevailing discursive order. Moreover, as observed by Lanzing, Chrysanthou and McQuire, these confessional self-disclosures become a means through which the self can be improved, perfected, or normalised. The next section turns to explore how certain legislative works to support the obedience of the individual to the regime of transparency.

Legislating for the transparent subject

One of the central functions of law to the discourse of transparency is to afford it legitimacy, and to, thus, legitimise efforts to force transparency on individuals where, otherwise, such efforts might be considered an unjust intrusion into the individual's private life. Two key laws are noted here which do just this. The first are laws which grant the state extended powers of surveillance, which I look at with respect to the Investigatory Powers Act of the UK. The second, and perhaps more complex, are laws which seek to normalise "open" behaviour and criminalise what is taken to be closed or secretive behaviour: that is, laws to ban the wearing of the Islamic veil in public spaces.

In 2016 the UK Houses of Parliament passed the Investigatory Powers Act (IPA), a law which come to have the nickname *The Snoopers Charter*. The IPA replaced the earlier Regulation of Investigatory Powers Act of 2000, particularly with respect to the use of online and digital based surveillance practices. The Act – which has been subject to legal challenges on the basis of human rights concerns with the use of mass surveillance powers – allows the state to monitor all communications data – including both content related data from web browsing history and communications, as well as meta-data, and provides for bulk interception powers. As Ni Loideain has articulated, the Act 'seeks to "avow" or put on a firm legal footing several known surveillance practices which have previously been shrouded in secrecy' (2018: 170). That the Act thus renders transparent the activities of the state in forcing transparency on individuals has little material consequences for limiting state surveillance in the first place (although of course the Act provides a mechanism through which the state can, arguably, be held accountable for actions which go beyond the legalised preview of surveillance, and perhaps a remedial cause of action for victims of unjust surveillance). More broadly, the Act legitimises a transparent society whereby its citizens must, in a reversal of the discourse of transparency's key conceit, be accountable to the state.

Another significant legislative avenue through which the state has pursued the enforcement of a transparent subject is through legislation that seeks to ban the wearing of the Islamic veil – niqab and burka – in public. In Europe, Germany, Austria, France, Belgium, The Netherlands, Italy, Spain, Turkey, Denmark, Russia, Switzerland and Bulgaria have all taken legislative steps to ban the wearing of the niqab and/or burka in public spaces. In France, women wearing the veil have even been detained after the law – *LOI No 2010-1192: Loi interdisant la dissimulation du visage dans l'espace public* (Law of 2010-1192: Act prohibiting concealment of the face in public space) came into force. Generally, a fine is administered for offenders, and in France, those caught in violation of the law must attend a citizenship course. While the matter raises serious concerns of freedom of religion and freedom of expression, it is also deeply rooted in modern society's ethos of what constitutes a good citizen. Many of the legal steps to ban the wearing of the veil in public arise from fears associated with terrorism and eve, supposedly, gender equality. Yet, more fundamentally, such actions arise from the normative and binary assumption that anything hidden or secretive is suspicious and deviant, and that which is in the open and transparent is intrinsically innocent and good.

Whistleblowing laws

Whistleblowing is considered a central component of a legislative regime for transparency, with Horne (2012) for example, stating that 'potentially the most powerful instruments for transparency in the public sector are whistleblowing and freedom of information arrangements' (392; see also Brown, Vandekerckhove & Dreyfus, 2014; Razak, Noor & Zakaria, 2015; Harwood, 2016). Broadly conceived, whistleblowing constitutes a disclosure of organisational wrongdoing by an individual (an employee) within the organisation. In South Africa, the legality of whistleblowing is set out under the Protected Disclosures Act (PDA). The Act, in the words of South Africa's National Anti-Corruption Forum 'draws heavily from the UK's Public Interest Disclosures Act' (PIDA), to set out the terms by which an individual can make a 'protected disclosure'. In keeping with the UK's PIDA, the PDA sets out four avenues through which an employee of an organisation (public and private) can make a disclosure regarding 'improprieties'[5] committed by its employer. These avenues include: first, confidential disclosure to a legal advisor (Section 5 PDA; Section 43D PIDA); second, disclosure to the employer (Section 6 PDA; Section 43C PIDA); third, where the employer is a public body, disclosure to a member of Cabinet or Executive Council (or Minister of the Crown in the UK) (Section 7 PDA; Section 43E PIDA); fourth, disclosure to a prescribed person or body (Section 8 PDA; Section 43F PIDA); and last, if the disclosure meets certain conditions,[6] a general disclosure can be made (that is, to the public).

While, whistle-blowing is often conceived as an act of resistance against powerful institutions, and is even regarded as politically subversive, the disclosures of 'truth' which transpire in the act of whistleblowing are both conditioned and normalised through the law.[7] Arguably, so too is the subjectivity of the whistle-blower in what Foucault might name her public *exomologesis*. In *On The Government of the Living*, Foucault describes exomologesis as designating

> An act that is intended to manifest both a truth and the subject's adherence to that truth; to make the exomologesis of one's belief is not just to assert what it is one believes, but to assert the fact of

believing; it is to make the act of assertion an object of assertion, and so to authenticate it either for oneself or before others.

(2014: 322)

Through public confession, or exomologesis, the subject not only binds themselves to the truth of what they proclaim, but also to the act of truth that they undertake and the consequences it may entail. However, for the whistle-blower, her act of truth is not so much a confession in the sense of a disclosure of personal information, but rather a public avowal of the transparency discourse itself, and its internationalisation within the subject-as-whistle-blower. Indeed, the whistle-blower reiterates the symbolic terms of the discourse of transparency through her act of disclosure, and thus re-legitimises transparency's central truth: that is, the truth of disclosure. What this analysis calls into question is the idea of whether the 'public interest' of whistleblowing lies not so much in the disclosure of what is disclosed, but in the very act of disclosure itself: a 'public interest' determined by the dominant order of which transparency is a part. Moreover, as the whistle-blower makes her public disclosure, she diverts the gaze of citizens onto her own disclosure, and away from their own acts of truth, as will be discussed below.

Depoliticising effects

In *On the Government of the Living* Foucault describes the interpellation of 'acts of truth' from the subject as 'government by the truth', which can effectively be understood as broad acceptance of the logic of discourse, thus that everyone obeys it (2014: 11–17). The fundamental objective of this 'rational art' of government is to engender a depoliticised State where both governor and governed are 'in agreement with' the truth (2014: 14). For Foucault, there will come a

utopian point in history when the empire of the truth will be able to make its order reign without the decisions of an authority or the choices of an administration having to intervene otherwise than as the formulation, obvious to everyone, of what is to be done.

(2014: 14)

To an extent, Foucault associates this new form of governance with late liberalism, and neoliberalism, and the inevitability in which these systems are presented (2008).

This 'empire of truth' about which Foucault speaks is normalising, seeking to eradicate difference and produce a homogenous society of subjects in agreement with the prevailing logic of truth and discourse. It is fundamentally depoliticising insofar as it refuses difference and dissent. Moreover, Foucault suggests a radical depoliticisation in the idea that 'truth' alone can govern; truth can take the place of government, requiring only its administrative function and negating the need for a political state as such. But the depoliticisation inherent here also extends to the subjectivities permitted through this 'empire of truth'. As Butler also explains, Foucault's ideas on 'government by the truth' encompass the foreclosure and delimitation of the possibilities of subjectivity, as the possible forms of self-constitution available to the subject are preordained by discourse (and its resultant régime of truth) (Butler, 2002).

In this sense, transparency represents not just an 'art of governing' which seeks to produce the manifestation of the truth of its discourse by its subjects, but is itself a resemblance of the depoliticisation inherent to the neoliberal project. The subject of transparency is required to conform to the truths of this discourse, not just through her acceptance of disclosed information as truth, but also in her manifestation of transparency through her own ethical open behaviour and through acts of truth, whether solicited through surveillance or surrendered through social media and self-tracking devices. Through such acts, the subject at once both constitutes herself as a subject of discourse, and reiterates its truth and legitimacy. Yet, moreover, transparency depoliticises – and within this depoliticisation, contains – the subject by foreclosing other possibilities of subjectivity that do not conform to its discourse, and by prescribing a general ethos of transparency to which all must aspire. As Han Byung Chul has noted, transparency 'leads to synchronisation and uniformity', engendering a 'compulsive conformity' (2015: vii-viii), which is decisively depoliticising. But of course something is lost here, not just in the uniformity of subjectivity that transparency enforces, but in the fact of openness itself. In an early critique of the transparency Jean-Jacques Rousseau sought to achieve as the ideal demeanour for an individual within society, Jean Starobinski concluded that a certain degree of secrecy, masking and opacity was central to subjectivity and the subjects relation to society (1988) (we will discuss this further in the following chapter with respect to Édouard Glissant's notion of the right to opacity).[8] But, too, the policing of subjectivity such that individuals are open and transparent, has critical implications for race and gender and other marginalised groups whose subjectivities are already considered problematic or, in Foucaultian terms, deviant within society. A good explication of this with respect to the maxim of our surveillant society – "nothing to hide" – with respect to gender and queer subjectivities includes the work of Kathryn Conrad (2009a,b), and with respect to race see Simone Browne's *Dark Matters: On the Surveillance of Blackness* (2015).

Additionally, in the act of becoming transparent, in the act of consciously manifesting transparency outwards, the subject is brought to bear on itself, and the effects of this inward refocusing can also be understood as depoliticising. In *Camera Lucida*, Roland Barthes deliberates upon the psychological effects of seeing oneself in a photographic image, locating it within a 'History of Looking' that remains pertinent for techniques of surveillance and watching that have become such an intrinsic function of the modern state:

> The photograph is the advent of myself as other: a cunning dissociation of consciousness from identity. [...] Today it is as if we repressed the profound madness of Photography; it reminds us of our mythic heritage only by that faint uneasiness which seizes me when I look at 'myself' on a piece of paper.
>
> (1981: 12–13)

For Barthes, photography fundamentally changed the way we look at ourselves. In looking at a photograph of himself, the subject sees his own subjectivity as object. Barthes' point here is not dissimilar to that put forward by Foucault at about the same time,[9] that through discourse – as an external ordering of society – the subject is objectivised (Barthes, 1981; Foucault, 2000: 326). Where Barthes's heautoscopy (to see a distanced figure of oneself) occurs through visceral interaction with a photograph, effecting only a doppelgänger moment of 'faint uneasiness' (1981: 14); for Foucault this moment signals the surrendering of the self under the order of discourse, and the loss of the subject's sovereign gaze. This is foreshadowed in his earlier work, *The Order of Things*, where he writes that 'our gaze disappears from ourselves at the moment of our actual looking' (1989: 4). As the gaze turns inward, a move which for Butler has always already taken place in the discursive constitution of the subject (1997: 2–20), the subject both recognises himself, and constitutes himself, as object. As he manifests and surrenders to discourse, the subject is depoliticised, insofar as other possibilities for other kinds of subjectivities have been foreclosed and delimited. The subject is now contained within the order of discourse.

The whistleblowing acts of Snowden and in the Cambridge Analytica matter mentioned in the introduction to this chapter, redirected the public's gaze upon the whistle-blower's own act of truth and called the public to witness perhaps not the spectacle but the *image* of transparency – its framed viewpoint. In the Snowden saga, as with other recent whistleblowing episodes (such as William Binney, Perry Fellwork, Ruce Tice, Mark Klein and Thomas Tamm) the framed viewpoint contains the reality of the collection of personal data by the state. Thus, what Snowden engendered was a heautoscopic ensemble whereby the public was called to gaze *upon* itself being gazed *at* by the state. However, if we concur with Slavoj Žižek's argument that very often such disclosures only reveal what we already know but do not wish to articulate as public knowledge (2011: 10), then the significance of whistleblowing lies not so much in what is revealed (as it is already known) but in the act of revelation itself: the significance of which entails both the reiteration of the symbolic terms of transparency through the whistle-blower's exomologesis, and the re-articulation of the depoliticised space of the transparent subject, whose knowledge of its acts of truth is concealed (or rendered invisible).

Summary

In *On the Government of the Living*, Foucault suggests that the relationship between the self, obedience, and truth – upon which his Christian archaeology in these lectures is focused – requires further analysis in relation to contemporary forms of governance (2014). In this chapter I have set out to undertake such an analysis. I have sought to analyse some of the 'point[s] of application and methods used' (Foucault, 2000: 239) in the creation of the transparent subject, demonstrating that the discourse of transparency interpellates acts of truth by which the individual is called upon to constitute her subjectivity in accordance with the dominant discourse of transparency. Within this paradigm, law functions as a vehicle through which the normative notions of transparency and openness can be legitimised and forced onto the subject. Moreover, I have shown how whistleblowing can be re-read as a public act of truth, through which the whistle-blower publically manifests and legitimises transparency's régime of truth.

Through its dominant discursive power transparency has become a normative category of being which forecloses and delimits other possibilities for subjectivity, the effects of which are – as I've discussed here – fundamentally depoliticising. In particular, the normative category of being is predicated around the maxim of "nothing to hide … nothing to fear". Yet, as Zuboff has pointed out, 'the real psychological truth is this: If you've got nothing to hide, then you are nothing' (2018: 479), as the form of subjectivity lies in the sacred, private and hidden aspects of human life. That efforts to mitigate the pervasive loss of privacy in modern digital society contain such exhaustive references to the need for transparency (the GDPR, for example, includes the right to transparency as a fundamental right of data subjects (Article 12)), further points to the depoliticising effects of its discourse, and is revealing of a moment I am calling the post-transparent: when transparency no longer points to anything but its own discursive logic and is heuristically moot.

Notes

1 With effect The Great Hack, Netflix 2019, traces the history of Cambridge Analytica and its role in the US Presidential Elections of 2016.
2 I take the notion of 'interpellation' from Althusser, who used it to describe the way in which 'ideological state apparatuses' call on the self, thus constituting their identity as subject (2001).
3 I draw my understanding of 'depoliticisation' in part from Burham, 2001.
4 See also, Elden, 2016.
5 The PDA sets out a list of 'improprieties' under its definition of 'disclosures', and includes:
   1 **Definitions**
   'disclosure' [...]

   (a) That a criminal offence has been committed, is being committed or is likely to be committed;
   (b) That a person has failed, is failing or is likely to fail to comply with any legal obligation to which that person is subject;
   (c) That a miscarriage of justice has occurred, is occurring or is likely to occur;
   (d) That the health or safety of an individual has been, is being or is likely to be endangered;
   (e) That the environment has been, is being or is likely to be damaged;
   (f) Unfair discrimination as contemplated in the Promotion of Equality and Prevention of Unfair Discrimination Act, 2000 (Act 4 of 2000); or
   (g) That any matter referred to in paragraphs (a) to (f) has been, is being or is likely to be deliberately concealed.

6 Conditions include that the employee has already disclosed the information to the employer, who has not acted upon it; or that the employee fears reprisal by the employer if the disclosure is made to a prescribed person; and that the disclosure contains a significant impropriety and is made in good faith and deemed to be true by the employee. Section 9 of the PDA; Section 43G of the PIDA.
7 On the normalising function of law see (Fitzpatrick, 2013: 53–59).
8 For a discussion on Starobinski's critique of transparency, see also Geroulanos, 2017.
9 Camera Lucida was first published in 1980, a period when Foucault was delivering his lectures at the College de France, many of which focused on the constitution of subjectivity.

Further reading

Althusser, L. 2001. Ideology and Ideological State Apparatuses. In L. Althusser *'Lenin and Philosophy' and Other Essays*. Trans. B. Brewster. New York: New York University Press, pp. 85–126.

80   *Towards the post-transparent*

Award, N. F., & Krishnan, M. S. 2006. The Personalization Privacy Paradox: An Empirical Evaluation of Information Transparency and the Willingness to be Profiled Online for Personalization. *MIS Quarterly* 30(1): 13–28.

Barthes, R. 1981. *Camera Lucida.* Trans. R. Howard. New York: Hill and Wang.

Birchall, C. 2015. Aesthetics of the Secret. *New Formations* 83: 25–46.

Brown, A. J., Vandekerckhove, W., & Dreyfus, S. 2014. The Relationship Between Transparency, Whistleblowing, and Public Trust. In P. Ala'i & R. G. Vaugn (eds). *Research Handbook on Transparency.* Chelterham: Edward Elgar Publishing, pp. 30–58.

Browne, S. 2015. *Dark Matters: On the Surveillance of Blackness.* Durham, NC: Duke University Press.

Burham, P. 2001. New Labour and the Politics of Depoliticisation. *The British Journal of Politics and International Relations* 3(2): 127–149.

Butler, J. 1997. *The Psychic Life of Power: Theories in Subjection.* Stanford, CA: Stanford University Press.

Butler, J. 2002. What is Critique: An Essay on Foucault's Virtue. In D. Ingram (ed). *The Political: Readings in Continental Philosophy.* Malden: Blackwell Publishers, pp. 212–226.

Chrysanthou, M. 2002. Transparency and Selfhood: Utopia and the Informed Body. *Social Science and Medicine* 54(3): 469–479.

Conrad, K. 2009a. "Nothing to Hide … Nothing to Fear": Discriminatory Surveillance and Queer Visibility in Great Britain and Northern Ireland. In N. Giffney & M. O'Rourke (eds). *Ashgate Research Companion to Queer Theory.* Surrey: Ashgate Publishing Ltd, chapter 19.

Conrad, K. 2009b. Surveillance, Gender and the Virtual Body in the Information Age. *Surveillance & Society* 6(4): 380–387.

Elden, S. 2005. The Problem of Confession: The Productive Failure of Foucault's History of Sexuality. *Journal for Cultural Research* 9(1): 23–41.

Elden, S. 2016. *Foucault's Last Decade.* Cambridge: Polity Press.

Fisher, E. 2014. Exploring the Legal Architecture of Transparency. In P. Ala'i & R. G. Vaugn (eds). *Research Handbook on Transparency.* Cheltenham: Edward Elgar Publishing, pp. 59–79.

Fitzpatrick, P. 2013. Foucault's Other Law. In B. Golder (ed). *Re-Reading Foucault: On Law, Power and Rights.* Abingdon: Routledge, pp. 39–63.

Foucault, M. 1971. Nietzsche, Genealogy, History. In P. Rabinow (ed). *The Foucault Reader.* New York: Pantheon Books, pp. 76–100.

Foucault, M. 1973. *The Birth of the Clinic.* Trans. A. Sheridan. London: Tavistock.

Foucault, M. 1977. The Political Function of the Intellectual. *Radical Philosophy* 17(13): 126–133.

Foucault, M. 1989. *The Order of Things.* London: Routledge.

Foucault, M. 1995. *Discipline and Punish: The Birth of the Prison.* Trans. A. Sheridan. Oxford: Vintage.

Foucault, M. 1998. *The Will to Knowledge: The History of Sexuality Volume 1.* Trans. R. Hurley. New York: Pantheon Books.

Foucault, M. 2000. The Subject and Power. In P. Rabinow (ed). *Power: Essential Works of Foucault 1954–1984 Volume 3.* New York: New Press, pp. 326–348.

Foucault, M. 2003. *'Society Must be Defended' Lecture Series at the Collège de France, 1975–76.* Trans. D. Macey. Basingstoke: Palgrave MacMillon.

Foucault, M. 2008. *The Birth of Biopolitics: Lectures at the Collège De France 1978–79.* Trans. G. Burchell. Basingstoke: Palgrave MacMillon.

Foucault, M. 2014. *On the Government of the Living: Lectures at the Collège de France 1979–1980.* Trans. G. Burchell. Basingstoke: Palgrave MacMillon.

France. 2010. *LOI No 2010-1192: Loi interdisant la dissimulation du visage dans l'espace public.*

Frischmann, B., & Selinger, E. 2018. *Re-Engineering Humanity.* Cambridge: Cambridge University Press.

Geroulanos, S. 2017. *Transparency in Postwar France: A Critical History of the Present.* Stanford, CA: Stanford University Press.

Harwood, W. H. 2016. Secrecy, Transparency and Government Whistleblowing. *Philosophy and Social Criticism* 43(2): 164–186.

Horne, S. 2012. Can I See Clearly Now? Public Sector Transparency and Disclosure Revisited. *Keeping Good Companies* 64(7): 392–396.

Lanzing, M. 2016. The Transparent Self. *Ethics and Information Technology* 18(1): 9–16.

McQuire, S. 2003. From Glass Architecture to Big Brother: Scenes from a Cultural History of Transparency. *Cultural Studies Review* 9(1): 103–123.

Ni Loideain, N. 2018. A Bridge Too Far? The Investigatory Powers Act and Human Rights Law. In L. Edwards (ed). *Law, Policy and the Internet* (2nd Edition). Bloomsbury: Hart, pp. 165–192.

Ni Loideain, N. Forthcoming 2020. *EU Data Privacy Law and Serious Crime: Data Retention and Policymaking.* Oxford: Oxford University Press.

Plaisance, P. L. 2007. Transparency: An Assessment of the Kantian Roots of a Key Element in Media Ethics Practice. *Journal of Mass Media Ethics* 22(2–3): 187–207.

Razak, S. N. A. A., Noor, W. N. B. W. M., & Zakaria, M. 2015. Breaking the Silence: The Efficacy of Whistleblowing in Improving Transparency. *Scientific Research Journal* 3(4): 35–39.

Republic of South Africa. 2000. Protected Disclosures Act, 26 of 2000.

Starobinski, J. 1988. *Jean-Jacques Rousseau, Transparency and Obstruction.* Chicago, IL: University of Chicago Press.

United Kingdom. 1998. Public Interest Disclosures Act 1998.

United Kingdom. 2000a. Protected Disclosures Act, 26 of 2000.

United Kingdom. 2000b. Regulation of Investigatory Powers Act, c. 23.

United Kingdom. 2016. Investigatory Powers Act, c. 26.

Žižek, S. 2011. Good Manners in the Age of WikiLeaks. *London Review of Books* 33(2): 9–10.

Zur, O., Williams, H. M., Lehavot, K., & Knapp, S. 2009. Psychotherapist Self-Disclosure and Transparency in the Internet Age. *Professional Psychology: Research and Practice* 40(1): 22–30.

Part III

Resistance

6   Resisting transparency

Introduction

'Not like that, not for that, not by them' (Foucault, 1997: 42). For Jean Baudrillard, as discussed in Chapter 4 of this book, there is no longer the possibility of resistance, for through his prophetic, radical and arguably nihilistic critique we reach an impasse and critique itself is exhausted. Baudrillard offers no further elucidations: the exchange of signs continues ad infinitum, and with it disappears, or disperses, other contingencies and possibilities within which any kind of resistance or repoliticisation can be kindled. However, this kind of thinking remains unproductive for imagining and creating a future where transparency is no longer so dominant, or the terms of its discourse have changed. Indeed, it is important to note that there have been instances where citizens have drawn on techniques of transparency, such as access to information laws, to hold institutions of power to account, and to resist injustices. The South African case of a local community seeking records through a Promotion of Access to Information Act application from ArcelorMittal, South Africa's largest steel producer, which demonstrated the environmental impact of their activities, can serve as an example here of resistance (2014). Yet, such cases remain exceptional to the normative discourse of transparency.

In this chapter I explore the notion of resistance as set out in Foucault's work before examining how the discourse of transparency has, and could be, resisted. As Foucault's thought on resistance is, arguably, under-theorised, yet remains a critical touchstone to his ideas of power, I begin by considering some of the other elements of his oeuvre which may provide us with a better understanding of what he could have meant by resistance. These elements are discourse, critique and his notion of dispositif developed in his later work in relation to the idea of governmentality. Following this, the chapter turns to examine the right to be forgotten as a possible legal avenue through which transparency could be conceived as being resisted, as well as other efforts to move towards an offline life. Lastly, I explore the work of Claire Birchall with respect to secrecy and opacity, and the possibilities for changing the symbolic terms on which transparency rests.

Foucault, power and resistance

The idea of resistance is central to Foucault's conception of power. In *The History of Sexuality Volume 1*, he writes: '[w]here there is power, there is resistance, and yet, or rather consequently, this resistance is never in a position of exteriority in relation to power' (1998: 95). Resistance works like a necessary by-product of power, both fuelling its continuation and allowing for the possibility that its effects could be undone. However, resistance remains an ambiguous and under-theorised idea within Foucaultian thought (Zizek, 1999; Golder & Fitzpatrick, 2009: 71–77). Is it the surplus of power? Can it work outside of disciplining power? Is it a term to describe an otherness which power can inhabit? Does it rest upon the inherent contingency of discourse and subjectivity? Further, in their analysis of Foucaultian thought, Dreyfus and Rabinow ask:

> [i]s there any way to resist the disciplinary society other than to understand how it works and to thwart it whenever possible? Is there a way to make resistance positive, that is, to move toward a 'new economy of bodies and pleasures?'
>
> (1982: 207)

Yet, if we accept that resistance is always already at work *in* power (for, as noted about, 'resistance is never in a position of exteriority in relation to power' (1998: 95), that it is a factor of power's relationality, then a number of Foucaultian concepts can be drawn upon to elucidate further on what resistance could mean. The first is discourse. Indeed, the central arguments of this book has been that the modern usage of transparency can be understood as a Foucaultian discourse. Yet, as a discourse, it is also inherently contingent, on the verge of being unhinged, and it is the task of critique to narrate discourse's contingency. Despite the iterative efforts of discourse to 'fix' meaning, a discourse is, as both Foucault's archaeological and genealogical analysis shows, subject to historical construction and reconstruction. And it is in this tension between a discourse's claim to a-historicity and universality, and its demonstrable construction by those in power, that resistance lies. Where this may begin to show the possibility of unfixing discursive truths and of resistance to the symbolic terms, or logic, of a discourse, the fact that its production – and particularly in the case of dominant discourses like transparency – takes place in the hands of the powerful and privileged becomes a critical sticking point in the realisation of the broader objectives of resistance to challenge the continuation of the current terms of the discourse. This therefore seems to suggest that the possibility of an alternate transparency can only arise when the neoliberal West cease holding its reigns.

The second Foucaultian notion we can draw on is that of critique. In his essay, 'What is Critique?' Foucault articulates a conception of 'critique' as relational to his notion of governmentality. Broadly, governmentality is an idea Foucault comes to in his later work to describe the way in which human behaviour as well as society and its institutions becomes subject to the governing forces of power, forces which predetermine what kind of behaviour, or category of being, is considered acceptable within society, and which is not (2000; 2004). He notes in an essay entitled 'Subject and Power' that *'to govern, in this sense, is to control the possible field of action of others' (2000: 341)*. The discussion in the previous chapter around the government of individuals through the truth, would fall under the ambit of his notion of governmentality. Thus, with respect to critique, Foucault writes:

> In this great preoccupation about the way to govern and the search for the ways to govern, we identify a perpetual question which would be: 'how not to be governed *like that*, by that, in the name of those principles, with such and such an objective in mind and by the means of such procedures, not like that, not for that, not by them'.
>
> (1997: 42)

This *search for* other realities and possibilities that have been supposedly foreclosed, and other ways of governing, is what constitutes 'critique'. The refusal, 'not like that, nor for that, not be them', constitutes what I see as the central force of resistance, a resistance that seems to constitute, at once, critique. Critique is, moreover, an ethical endeavour as it works to disturb our given moral order and to question the locus of truth and morality against which our present reality is measured. And, given that genealogical critique emanates from within the practices and conditions which are its object of study, it can – too – be understood as 'resistance', that is, as a by-product of governmental power.

The last Foucaultian concept I wish to discuss here as an avenue for thinking through what resistance could, conceptually, mean is Foucault's idea of *dispositif*. The idea of *dispositif* arose within Foucault's later works, particularly *Security, Territory, Population* (2004) where Foucault critiques a *dispositif* of security; and in an interview on the second instalment of *History of Sexuality* where he discusses the notion of a *dispositif* of sexuality (1980). The idea can be loosely understood as the genealogical counterpart to the episteme of archaeology, insofar as *dispositif* represents a relational and historically situated dynamic between different societal structures, including institutions and discourses, just as episteme represented the structural relationship between discourses within a specific historical epoch (Dreyfus & Rabinow, 1982: 121). In its particularities, Foucault articulated in the 1977 'The Confession of the Flesh' interview three discernible elements the *dispositif*. First, it encompasses both the discursive and the non-discursive, thus marking a clear move beyond the archaeological (1997: 196–197). Second, it describes a heterogeneous relationality of power which works across various 'elements' (1997: 194), whether discursive or otherwise. And third, it bears a strategic function as it responds to – yet in its relationality, also produces – a particular moment (1997: 194). Thus, whereas governmentality is the overall rationality of governing which works across various domains of discourse, the *dispositif* is the assemblage of power relations which facilitates the acceptance or rejection of statements within a particular discourse based on the categories of reason predetermined by the governmentality, and thereby *producing the discursive moment itself.* Indeed, as Foucault notes, within a *dispositif*

> a particular discourse can figure at one time as the programme of an institution, and at another it can function as a means of justifying or masking a practice which itself remains silent, or as a secondary re-interpretation of this practice, opening out for it a new field of rationality.
>
> (1997: 194)

The notion of *dispositif* is instructive for understanding the workings of resistance. Dreyfus and Rabinow articulate that the *dispositif* is both 'the method of the effective historian as well as the structure of the cultural practices he is examining' (1982: 121). Indeed, within this concept – which names the heterogeneous, relational and strategic field of power in which discourses are put to work at a given point in time and space – is the idea of resistance itself. As above, the critique of the genealogist forms part of the *dispositif* itself. Thus, the critique on transparency I am putting forward here is in fact already embedded within the *dispositif* of the governmentality in which transparency functions. Yet moreover, and recalling Foucault's play on the idea of genealogy as a kind of 'parody' in his essay 'Nietzsche, Genealogy, History' (1971), the critique of this book stands as a kind of resistance-as-parody of transparency as it works to *reveal* or *disclose* that which is hidden in transparency's construction.

Resistance to transparency

There are, of course, myriad ways in which the discourse of transparency has been, and continues to be, resisted. Whether that involves state of the so-called Global South taking on the idea of transparency on their own terms, and assimilating it within local governance values, or whether that involves movements towards an undocumented life through efforts to retract oneself from the modern dependency on digital technologies. Much as the discourse of transparency ash permeated throughout many parts of the world and many different aspects of life, there will be equally many different ways through which resistance to its dominance can be enacted. For Michel de Certeau, Luce Giard and Peirre Moyal, who explore the ways in which individuals creatively resist dominant structures within modern life, orality presents an opportunity to move away from and resist the dominance of technologies of writing and text to which modern subjectivities are tied (1998). This may be one way to think about how to resist the technologies of transparency imposed on the individual through their use of technology which tracks and monitors their every move (as discussed in the previous chapter). Indeed, the social movement against technology and towards a greater offline society – the techlash movement (Heaven, 2018) – constitutes one such example of how the hegemony of transparency through digital technologies could be resisted.

The way in which online digital systems generate and collect personal data, and through the same nodes and points of application both prod and regulate human behaviour, interests and even knowledge, is a ready example of the *dispositif* of the power of surveillance capitalism (Zuboff, 2018) at work. Thus, any efforts to move offline, as noted above, constitute resistance to the minute apparatuses and workings of power. However, as Zuboff is quick to point out:

> Individuals each wrestling with the myriad complexities of their own data protection will be no match of surveillance capitalism's

staggering asymmetries of knowledge and power. If the past two decades have taught us anything, it is that the individual alone cannot bear the burden of this fight at the new frontier of power.

(2018: 492)

Thus, to resist through offline movements would require collective and not individual action alone. It would also require access to what Zuboff describes as the shadow text, noted in Chapter 4, such that the objectives and gains of this digital order could be understood and ultimately challenged.

Within a legal framework, one of the ways in which the transparency imposed on the individual through digital technologies can be seen as potentially resisted is through the so-called right to be forgotten, established under the European Union General Data Protection Regulation (GDPR, 2016). The right to be forgotten arose out of the matter of *Google Spain SL, Google Inc v Angecia Española de Protección de Datos, Mario Costeja González* heard by the Court of Justice of the European Union. In 2014 the Court passed down its decision that search engines retain responsibility for the processing of personal information that derives from search results, and that, where requested a search engine must consider applications for the removal of certain results and links pertaining to the individual's history and personal information. The Court ensured that a wide berth of possible grounds for a deletion of personal information request, with the non-exhaustive definition that results 'appear to be inadequate, irrelevant or no longer relevant or excessive in light of the time that had elapsed' (CJEU, 2014: para 92). At the time of the decision, the GDPR had not been finalised and it was recommended that a data subject right fitting for a request for removal of personal information from a search engine be included within its ambit. An express "right to be forgotten" was not included, but instead the right to erasure was established (GDPR, 2016, Article 17). This right both expands and limits the scope of what the CJEU laid out in 2014. It provides for data subjects to request that their personal data be deleted by a data controlled, so in this respect the right expands the CJEU's decision beyond simply search engines. However, the GDPR provides a series of specific grounds upon which a request for deletion can be made, which are arguably more limiting than that originally set out by the CJEU. These grounds include: that the information is no longer needed for the original purpose for which it was collected; the data subject withdraws their consent for the processing of their data, if there are not other legal grounds for which the data is being processed; the data subject objects to their data being processed (which includes being held) and there are no other legitimate reasons other-wise; or if the personal data has been processed unlawfully (GDPR, 2016: Article 17). However, the reality of achieving digital erasure or of being forgotten are, as Judith Townend glibly notes, 'something a bit different from what the law is trying to achieve' (2017: 31). More critically, Townend points out that the concept is legally and ethically problematic (2017). Indeed, practically speaking, to exercise this right to erasure requires a prior understanding of the intricacies of what has generally been recognised as a highly complex piece of legislation. Like the concerns raised with access to information requests in Chapter 2, this avenue for redress or even resistance, will only be accessible to those with the means and know-how to realise it.

Another concept through which resistance to transparency has been imagined, and that similarly draws on the legal terminology of "rights", is Édouard Glissant's notion of the right to opacity, discussed, in particular, by Clare Birchall (2015a,b).[1] Glissant was a Martiniquan poet and philosopher whose thought on the right to opacity is largely found in his work of 1989 *Poetics in Relation*. For Birchall, Glissant's right to opacity entails the 'right to not be reduced to, or rendered comprehensible/transparent by the dominant, Western filian-based order' (2015b: 203). Glissant's idea – which is inherently concerned with the othering at play in the epistemic violence (Spivak) of Western knowledge – calls for a rejection of the need to understand, and thus re-duce, all matters and people. Instead we must allow for the complexity and irreducibility that is humanity as a central tenant of ethical living. With respect to transparency, Birchall writes that 'the ethical subject is more aligned with secrecy than transparency in Glissant's writing in a way that offers us an alternative to the moral certitude of the 'trans-parency movement' and the idea of the 'good' neoliberal data subject' (2015b: 204). Indeed, the notion of complexity that Glissant advocates stands as a critical antithesis to the simplicity and simplification of so-ciety that transparency seeks to impose (as discussed in Chapter 4 with reference to the illusion of transparency) and that can only be achieved through its hegemonic and totalitarian realisation.

To change the symbolic terms of the discourse, and work to cherish and value notions that the discourse of transparency have presented as problematic, provides another way to think through how the dominance of this discourse can be resisted. In addition to exploring ideas of opac-ity, Birchall has engaged with the idea of the secret and secrecy as an alternative strategy in countering the value statements made by trans-parency against these notions. For Birchall, transparency in fact holds a dialectic relationship to secrecy, particularly in regard to what she terms 'the politics of the secret', which she explores through a Derridean critique of transparency as différance (2015a: 45). In an earlier article, Birchall explores this contention through Jacque Derrida's deconstructive reasoning on the 'right to the secret' (2005). For Derrida, the secret is both withheld and promises a deferred truth, the arrival [*avenir*] of something to come, and therefore the possibility of something different to the current symbolic order of power (Derrida, 2006; Birchall, 2011). For Derrida, the 'secret' is simultaneously both formless and that which gives form; it is both that which 'impassions' community and communication, but which remains un-communicable (2001). Understood as such, Birchall calls for politics to strategically inhabit the tensions between 'transparency' and 'secrecy' as two symbiotic phenomena (2015a). She also considers the political possibilities inherent in the 'secret as secret' – rather than as a secret which has revealed itself – turning to artistic descriptions of the concept in order to grapple with its historical and cultural condition, and map out its political potential (2015a: 25). In all, Birchall's work – as briefly described here – works through the possible contingencies of meaning that the discourse of transparency seeks so fundamentally to fix.

Summary

In this chapter we have explored what resistance to the dominant discourse of transparency might both mean and look like. Noting the limitations of Foucault's work to provide a detailed theory of resistance, this chapter has begun by exploring three related aspects of Foucault's oeuvre from which a further understanding of resistance can be drawn: critique, *dispositif* and discourse. Critically, resistance can be understood as both a by-product of power which works through the same apparatus in which power operates, and, too, relational. In turning to the ways in which transparency has been resisted, I have examined efforts to move offline, and legal remedies including the right to be forgotten. In relation to the idea of discourse and the task of critique to unhinge discourse's inevitability and to show it to be contingent, I have also explored the work of Clare Birchall with respect to opacity and secrecy, as an effort to rethink and shift the symbolic terms of the discourse.

Note

1 Glissant's notion of the right to opacity is also discussed by Blas, 2016 and Simek, 2016.

Further reading

Birchall, C. 2011. The Politics of Opacity and Openness: Introduction to Transparency. *Theory, Culture and Society* 28(7–8): 7–25.

Birchall, C. 2015a. Aesthetics of the Secret. *New Foundations* 83: 25–46.

Birchall, C. 2015b. Data.gov–in–a–box: Delimiting Transparency. *European Journal of Social Theory* 18: 185–202.

Blas, Z. 2016. Opacities: An Introduction. *Camera Obscura* 92(2): 149–153.

Company Secretary of Arcelormittal South Africa and Another v Vaal Environmental Justice Alliance (69/2014) [2014] ZASCA 184; 2015 (1) SA 515 (SCA); [2015] 1 All SA 261 (SCA) (26 November 2014).

de Certeau, M., Giard, L., & Mayol, P. 1998. *The Practices of Everyday Life, Vol 2: Living and Cooking.* Trans. T. J. Tomasik. Minneapolis: University of Minnesota Press.

Derrida, J. 2001. I Have a Taste for the Secret. In J. Derrida & M. Ferraris (eds). *A Taste for the Secret.* Cambridge: Polity Press, pp. 1–92.

Derrida, J. 2005. The Last of the Rogue States: The 'Democracy to Come', Opening in Two Turns. In J. Derrida (ed). *Rogues: Two Essays on Reason.* Stanford, CA: Stanford University Press, pp. 232–341.

Dreyfus, H. L., & Rabinow, P. 1982. *Michel Foucault: Beyond Structuralism and Hermeneutics.* Chicago, IL: Chicago University Press.

Heaven, D. 2018. Techlash. *New Scientist* 237(3164): 28–31.

Foucault, M. 1971. Nietzsche, Genealogy, History. In P. Rabinow (ed). *The Foucault Reader.* New York: Pantheon Books, pp. 76–100.

Foucault, M. 1980. The Confessions of the Flesh. In C. Gordon (ed). *Power/ Knowledge: Selected Interviews and Other Writings.* New York: Pantheon Books, pp. 194–228.

Foucault, M. 1997. What is Critique? In *The Politics of Truth.* Trans. L. Hochrith & C Porter. Los Angeles: Semiotext(e), pp. 41–82.

Foucault, M. 1998. *The Will to Knowledge: The History of Sexuality Volume 1.* Trans. R. Hurley. New York: Pantheon Books.

Foucault, M. 2000a. The Subject and Power. In P. Rabinow (ed). *Power: Essential Works of Foucault 1954–1984 Volume 3.* New York: New Press, pp. 326–348.

Foucault, M. 2000b. The Ethics of the Concern of the Self as a Practice of Freedom. In P. Rabinow (ed). *Ethics: Subjectivity and Truth: Essential Words of Foucault 1954–1984 Volume 1.* New York: New York Press, pp. 281–302.

Foucault, M. 2004. *Security, Territory, Population: Lectures at the Collège de France 1977–1978.* Trans. G. Burchell. Basingstoke: Palgrave MacMillon.

Glissant, E. 1997. *Poetics of Relation.* Trans. B. Wing. Ann Arbour: Michigan University Press.

Golder, B., & Fitzpatrick, P. 2009. *Foucault's Law.* Abingdon: Routledge.

Regulation (European Union). 2016. 2016/679 of the European Parliament and of the Council of 27 April 2016 on the Protection of Natural Persons with Regard to the Processing of Personal Data and on the Free Movement of Such Data, and Repealing Directive 95/46/EC [2016] OJ L119/1 (GDPR).

Simek, N. 2015. Stubborn Shadows. *Posthumanisms* 23(1–2): 363–373.

Townend, J. 2017. Data Protection and the 'Right To Be Forgotten' in Practice: A UK Perspective. *International Journal of Legal Information* 45(1): 28–33.

Žižek, S. 1999. *The Ticklish Subject: The Absent Centre of Political Ontology.* London: Verso.

Zuboff, S. 2018. *The Age of Surveillance Capitalism: The Fight for a Human Future at the New Frontier of Power.* London: Profile Books.

Conclusion

> But what is philosophy today – philosophical activity, I mean – if it
> is not the critical work that thought brings to bear on itself? In what
> does it consist, if not in the endeavour to know how and to what extent
> it might be possible to think differently, instead of legitimating what
> is already known?
>
> (Foucault, 1984: 8–9)

Michel Foucault memorably began the first chapter of *The Order of
Things* with a detailed commentary on Las Meninas, Diego Velázquez's
17th-century painting in Madrid's Museo del Prado (1989: 6). For
Foucault, the painting represents the intersection between two epis-
temes – the Classical and the modern – and the place of humankind, as
both a knowing subject and as the subject of knowledge, within them.
He sees the characters of the painting captured in a moment of cho-
reographic suspense: some made visible and others invisible. Notably,
Velázquez himself features in the painting in an instance of mirrored
visibility; while the subject of his painting (the King) is left outside
of the frame. Yet, in making himself visible in the painting, the real
Velázquez is both hidden and forgotten through his own representation. Meanwhile, the implicit positioning of the King estranges us – as
the real spectators of the painting – who, in sitting with the King outside of the frame, realise our own invisibility and misplacement. This
scene constructs a representation of how humankind has become at
once the knowing subject, constructing the knowledge of what he sees,
and the subject of knowledge, as what he sees is himself and his own
subjectivity, externally fashioned.

Almost 50 years after *The Order of Things* was published, Edward
Snowden made what is arguably a similar conceit in disclosing
details of the collection and storage of personal information by

government agencies. Through his disclosure, Snowden called upon the public to witness the construction of their subjectivity by the State: to witness the gaze of the State upon us. Just as the painted Velázquez looks out from the painting, the gaze of the data-collecting State returns its stare. We are looking at ourselves being looked at: the gaze makes a double-turn inward. Snowden's disclosure marked a critical turning point in the public's knowledge around how, and how much, their data was being collected and stored by government agencies (Ni Loideain, 2020). More recently, the Cambridge Analytica case of 2018 – where the data analytics company used profiling based on Facebook data and targeted advertising to influence outcomes, such as the 2016 US election – became another historical moment in the public's understanding of how our data is used to budge or manipulate behaviour and decisions, but also, how we contribute to the information society and transparency discourse through the constant submission of personal information online (what Zuboff (2018) calls the "first text" – see Chapter 4). How we are both is knowing subject, with our vague and partial understanding of the system – revealed through episodes like Snowden's revelation and the Cambridge analytical standards, and its subject of knowledge, as our data is produced and collected, and our knowledge of the world prompted and controlled through algorithmic search ordering, filter bubbles and even fake news.

That the discourse of transparency would be invoked on the bodies of its subject was, perhaps, always foreshadowed. For the idea of transparency necessitates its full realisation, as anything less than complete visible clarity would be opacity. But the consequences of this drive for total transparency are significant. For John Roberts, this means that 'transparency works to advertise an ideal against which we will always fail' (2009: 959). For Rachel Hall it means the end of communication as, within a totally transparent society that which can or needs to be communicated, is already known by the receiving subject (2007: 321). And for Stefanos Geroulanos, 'any effort to enforce absolute transparency – on oneself, others, or society at large – was bound to fail and primed to recreate, perhaps in a far more paranoid form, the very shadows and masks it sought to banish' (2017: 7). In this book, we have seen how the quest for total transparency is both a part of the internal logic of its discourse, proselytised around the world and, moreover, materialises on the bodies of citizens and individuals who are hailed to be transparent through surveillance technologies and other mechanisms of our digital milieu. But that this drive for total transparency and its coupling with the digital and informational transformations that have characterised our late modernity, has led, too, to transparency's unfolding. As the call for and cherishment of transparency has intensified in response to informational crises such as disinformation (Chapter 4) and the loss of data privacy and control (Chapter 5), transparency's fallacies are beginning to be revealed. No longer can it be assumed that information released and received in the public domain is true, real or objective. No longer can transparency be assumed to foster trust in institutions and strengthen democracy. No longer can it be assumed that the society we live in can be understood and accessed by those who do not hold the reins of power. That the fallacies of transparency are coming undone marks what I have called here the post-transparent: a society where the call to transparency continues, but its claims cannot be realised, in part because transparency has already been achieved and its realisation has been definitively opaque.

This book has intended to break the totality of transparency's discourse by, as in the epithet above, 'thinking differently, instead of legitimating what is already known' (Foucault, 1984: 8–9) or said. I have sought to contribute to the burgeoning school of thought on transparency, and open up new questions about its relationship to the general politics of truth and modes of subjectivity connected to this idea within modern society. I draw on Foucaultian thought to articulate my concerns with the modern notion of transparency, building a genealogy of the concept which encompasses a critique of its historical emergence and truth claims; the construct of its discourse; the strategies of power through which it is put to work; and its effects on subjectivity and the body. Within this context, I have described discourse broadly as a set of prescriptive ideas which structure the way in which we see and think about the world. Indeed, it is hoped that this critique, as Foucault put it, 'incites new reactions, and induces a crisis in the previously silent behaviour, habits, practices, and institutions' (2001: 74) of transparency. By drawing on both the archaeological and genealogical analytics developed by Foucault, I have, instead, approached transparency sceptically, seeking to disturb its dominant position. In short, I have sought to *re*-politicise a concept whose effects I have shown to be *de*-politicising, and in doing so, to show that the effort of critique itself forms a practice of resistance against the dominant discourse (Chapter 6).

This book has detailed how the construction of the discourse of transparency has taken place and analysed its transformation and distribution. I began by tracing the entrance of transparency into discourse from its early iterations in the camera and in glass architecture, to its rise as a metaphor following the designs for the League of

Nations building in the mid-20th century (Chapter 1). As I describe in Chapter 2, towards the end of the 20th century the discourse of transparency began to gain unquestionable legitimacy through the enactment of access to information laws and its associated with human rights. What these early indications of transparency fervently promoted was the idea that the concept was, if not an express human right to begin with, a value closely associated with human rights and all that came with it. Moreover, this propinquity to human rights provides transparency with a claim to being a neutral, universal and inclusive value – relevant for all people, everywhere. Indeed, I have sought to show that the critical function of the discourse of transparency is to hide its politics, to present the idea as a-political. Neutral, universal and without history. Presented thus, transparency becomes unquestionable.

It is thus that within modern society the idea of transparency has become a dominant centre, from which other realities are seen to deviate. Indeed, transparency is a powerful sign, loaded with particular powerful values which hold the ability to create and to shape other phenomena to which they are associated. As a discourse, transparency rests on a number of pre-conceived (and Western) categories of reason in order to outwardly project itself as universal (inclusive) and natural (*a priori*). One of the most powerful of these is the idea of democracy. As such, the discourse of transparency has sought, through the re-iteration of its statements, to fix the meaning of democracy, such that a State which does not make a claim to transparency is considered both undemocratic and illegitimate. But, simultaneously, this gives the transparency discourse its raison d'être (in the words of Alan Duncan of the UK Government) 'to improve' (United Kingdom, House of Commons, 2010) and to be proselytised upon States which have not, as yet, declared their commitment to the ideals of transparency (and particularly the African region) through a process of what I have spoken of as epistemic violence.

As I set out to divide the 'unitary discourse' of transparency as it is presented (Foucault, 2004: 11), my critique raises questions that are beyond the scope of this book to adequately address. One of these questions concerns the status of the concept of 'accountability' within the discursive strategy of transparency, as one of the key ideas often coupled with transparency. Moreover, one of the critical ways in which transparency is being put to work in our global society is as a justification for increased State security. There are a number of significant studies that have been conducted on this issue, including Rachel Hall's critique of 'the aesthetics of transparency in the war on terror' (2007).

Indeed, it is a matter which holds relevance particularly in light of Foucault's posthumously published lecture series: notably *Birth of Biopolitics*,[1] *Society must be Defended* (2003) and *Security, Territory, Population*, (2004) where he discusses issues of state sovereignty and security amidst the emergence of neoliberal forms of government. Another important concern is that of intellectual property and its place within the discursive regime of transparency as the effective monetisation of secrecy. In Slavoj Žižek's comments on the role of intellectual property and privatised knowledge, he suggests that it represents an immanent crisis in to modern capitalism (2012), a provocation that certainly merits of exploration with regard to its relationship to notions of openness.

Lastly, the other major line of enquiry that is raised here regards the differential experience of informational crises such as disinformation and privacy – or the production of the transparency subject – in the Global South, as compared to the Global North, where the attention of this book has been focused. This enquiry merits a book on its own and constitutes my current research project.

Note

1 Foucault *The Birth of Biopolitics: Lectures at the Collège De France 1978–79* (note 6 above).

Further reading

Foucault, M. 1984. *The Use of Pleasure, Volume 2 of the History of Sexuality*. Trans. R. Hurley. New York: Vintage Books.

Foucault, M. 1989. *The Order of Things*. London: Routledge.

Foucault, M. 2001. *Fearless Speech*. Ed J. Pearson. Los Angeles: Semiotext(e).

Foucault, M. 2003. *'Society Must Be Defended' Lecture Series at the Collège de France, 1975–76*. Trans. D. Macey. Basingstoke: Palgrave MacMillon.

Foucault, M. 2004. *Security, Territory, Population: Lectures at the Collège de France 1977–1978*. Trans. G. Burchell. Basingstoke: Palgrave MacMillon.

Foucault, M. 2008. *The Birth of Biopolitics: Lectures at the Collège De France 1978–79*. Trans. G. Burchell. Basingstoke: Palgrave MacMillon.

Hall, R. 2007. Of Ziploc Bags and Black Holes: The Aesthetics of Transparency in the War on Terror. *The Communication Review* 10(4): 319–349.

Ni Loideain, N. Forthcoming 2020. *EU Data Privacy Law and Serious Crime: Data Retention and Policymaking*. Oxford: Oxford University Press.

Roberts, J. 2009. No One Is Perfect: The Limits of Transparency and an Ethic for 'Intelligent' Accountability. *Accounting, Organizations and Society* 34(8): 957–970.

United Kingdom, House of Commons, International Development Committee. 2010. *The World Bank: 4th Report of Session 2010–11, Volume 1*, HC 606. Minutes of 23 November 2010 of International Development Committee, Evidence 5.

Žižek, S. 2012. The Revolt of the Salaried Bourgeoisie. *London Review of Books* 34(2): 9–10.

Zuboff, S. 2018. *The Age of Surveillance Capitalism: The Fight for a Human Future at the New Frontier of Power*. London: Profile Books.

Index

For Product Safety Concerns and Information please contact our EU
representative GPSR@taylorandfrancis.com
Taylor & Francis Verlag GmbH, Kaufingerstraße 24, 80331 München, Germany